2/8°

T5-BBZ-670

# BEASTS
# and
# BATTLES

## Fact in Legend and History?

# BEASTS
# And
# BATTLES

## Fact in Legend
## and History?

## by
## Hugh H. Trotti

RIVERCROSS PUBLISHING, INC.
NEW YORK, NEW YORK

Library of Congress Cataloging-in-Publication Data

Trotti, Hugh H.
    Beasts and battles : fact in legend and history / by Hugh H.
Trotti.
        p.    cm.
    Includes bibliographical references.
    ISBN 0-944957-04-8 : $18.95
    1. History, Ancient--Miscellanea.  2. Folklore and history.
3. Military history, Ancient--Miscellanea.  I. Title.
D62.T76  1989
930--dc20                                              89-24281
                                                          CIP

# CONTENTS

# DRAWINGS

# PREFACE

This book represents an effort to discover some historical reality behind the shifting shadows of the stories we receive from the past. This may be possible in some few cases, though certainly not in all; the effort should be worthwhile, though not especially fashionable.

We are in the odd position of sometimes knowing more about certain facts of the ancient world than did the ancient peoples themselves, and then again confronting areas of which we know nothing. Modern geographical knowledge is one example of our advantage, but we may never have full knowledge of ancient religious belief in some contexts. In the geographical area, the contention that Aristotle may have confused the river Araxes with the river Jaxartes (Syr-Darya) in A. B. Bosworth's recent *Conquest and Empire: The Reign of Alexander the Great* (New York: Cambridge University Press, p. 109), seems to demonstrate a confusion similar to that of Herodotus earlier—as we noted in our Chapter 3. I wish to thank J. Richard Greenwell for permission to use material submitted previously to the annual journal *Cryptozoology*, Vol. 7, 1988. Thanks also to Ed Oram, former editor of the *Georgia Skeptic* newsletter, where some of the author's condensed historical articles were published.

# BEASTS
# and
# BATTLES

### Fact in Legend and History?

# ▶ 1 ◀

# VAMPIRE KNIGHT

The darkness of prehistoric obscurity lies coiled about things we wish we knew, and like a magical mist it retreats before us only a little, enticing us onward. It seems odd that we know more of the past than did people of prior times. They lacked the skills of the science of our era. And it is also odd that mankind's puzzles do not evaporate at the historic benchmark of the introduction of writing and literacy. We seem to have more to puzzle over since we have begun keeping records; we have gathered a regular library of oddities, puzzles, and almost incomprehensible descriptions of events, creatures, and manifestations of a seemingly unlimited range of types. Our stories of strange or interesting things down through the ages since writing first began have worked to increase our wonder; instead of answering our questions, our records sometimes leave us in perplexity.

Some things that make us wonder are doubtless well understood by scholars, who may have overlooked the simplicity of our unvoiced questions, and so failed to provide explanations easily produced by them, but out of reach for some of us. It is the hope of this writer that he may shed some amount of light upon some few and simple questions by citing knowledge already obtained, and even bring forward some original thoughts upon some of the matters that follow.

Sometimes it all depends on how you look at things: what preconceptions you bring to a subject. For instance, on the subject of the "Origin of Cooking", an anthropologist might speculate that

# Beasts and Battles

it came from the offering of meat to a Fire God in the long-lost ages of mankind's infancy. Common Sense may say that it was simpler: did you ever attempt to eat meat that was frozen solid (during the last Ice Age, for example)? But both of these approaches may be wrong—the student of what might be called "paleoanthropology" would probably cite the occurence of fires on the grasslands which left behind "cooked" creatures for early people to eat. Such fires occur naturally, but people could learn from them. Indeed, more recent hunter-gatherers sometimes set such fires themselves, to "flush out" game (or, as a recent TV show about Australian aborigines related, for religious or mythic reasons). Of course, nobody really knows the "true" answer.

No one can be blamed for carrying the wrong preconceptions to the study of a subject, although as an ideal one could wish to extend one's "mental set" or even accumulate additional and differing "mental sets" for wholeness of judgment. This is accomplished by scholars who study our prehistoric ancestors by research methods involving many different fields. They gather to study the same subject, and as a result we should have a more well-rounded and detailed picture of that subject than if it had been approached from one direction or viewpoint.

To a person with a quite limited "mental set", many things outside of his area of interest might well appear marvels—or at least puzzling. But sometimes even a slight knowledge of one subject area may bring insights that link together or explain things that at first appear very different. It could be, for instance, that certain electrical phenomena may be called upon to explain two very different subjects of debate: one an ancient story, and the other an attribute of certain historic sites.

Now, we will admit that strange things exist, and some have not been explained in a satisfactory manner in today's world. But the more unknown or "strange" subjects often tend to attract unidirectional viewpoints or approaches. The priest may see a miracle, while the Flying Saucer buff sees a "UFO" in certain anomalous accounts. The following two such subjects are not best explained by the "Unidentified Flying Object" hypothesis, at least, but probably by rare natural events.

To those with that "mental set" or preference of belief, Moses and his Burning Bush is an example of the confrontation of a man with a "UFO"—is it really a clear account of such? Actually, the description probably is a clear account of something else, and in itself is quite plausible. The phenomenon called "Saint Elmo's Fire" comes to mind. Better known in the days of the sailing Clipper Ships and before, this "fire" was a strange fiery light that sometimes played about the masts and spars of ships—a fire that did not burn or destroy things, and left no damage. Here, then, a description that seems at first glance "miraculous" or at the very least unlikely, is reduced to a possible real physical phenomenon: (a rare, but known, electrical event).

Some believers in UFOs at all costs and in all places have yet another case to show. It is a real mystery that has been debated in recent years. Did UFO attackers "zap" prehistoric stone-walled hill-forts in the British Isles and elsewhere? Some of these forts, located on the tops of hills in Scotland and encircled by stone walls, display evidence of fused rocks in their walls. "Vitrified" by ray-shooting UFO attackers say some people. Experiments of a serious nature have been carried out in which masses of wood piled against duplicate walls failed to produce enough heat to fuse the rock except when exceptional amounts of wood were used—amounting to "over-kill". And yet the real ancient iron-age structures were really there, and really did exhibit fused or vitrified stones. (The piling of wood against the walls was not a likely tactic of more mundane prehistoric attackers, unless there had originally been wooden walls above the stone walls below.) The obvious answer to this puzzle would seem to be lightning strikes through the ages. (One description of this puzle—without UFOs—may be found in pp. 58-62 of Welfare and Fairley's *Arthur C. Clarke's Mysterious World*, A & W Publishers, New York, 1980, containing a preferred theory of fire from attackers, but admitting that puzzles remain. The text's second theory of accidental destructions also seems not quite adequate.) The stone walls were bound together with logs, but this practice is well-known in the builders of prehistoric walled forts. The Roman armies had encountered such structures and believed that bracing with wood and earth made the walls strong against attack by battering ram.

The last quarter of the eleventh century saw European warlords in the process of consolidating gains in Italy and striving to carve out kingdoms for themselves of larger area at the expense of the Byzantine Empire or the Arabs. Some were from Normandy, though called "Franks" by the people of the remaining Byzantine

# Beasts and Battles

Empire (who called themselves "Romans", as they were the remaining Eastern Roman Empire at a time when the Western Empire had fallen some six hundred years ago). One Norman to venture south to try his fortune was Robert Guiscard, a Duke of an Italian area now. He had a son named Bohemond, a man of war whose career was a great nuisance that brought difficulties and some danger to the Byzantines.

His father, Robert, warred against the Byzantines continually, and the son as well. It was even believed by the Byzantines that Bohemond held the aim in life of conquering Constantinople and gaining control of the Empire. It was not an unusual thing for "Franks" (also called "Latins" by the Greek Church peoples of Constantinople), to make war in any direction that might gain them land or kingdom of their own; they would fight with Christian or Saracen or anyone else for the purpose. The Crusades were often an excuse for taking loot or capturing land as much as a religious activity. The land in Italy that the knights from the north had taken and held had been Byzantine holdings.

Worse was to come, for the "Franks" made war even nearer to the Byzantines as often as they could, the Greek Christians being as much a target as Arabs. And Bohemond had made promises not kept to the Byzantine Emperor, involving the capture of places previously Byzantine but now Islamic. Such places were by agreement (as the Byzantines thought), to be turned over to the Byzantine Emperor—but were not handed over as expected.

Much territory had already been lost to the expansion of Islam, and the Byzantine hold upon other territories near the borders of its area of influence was shaky and subject to dispute. Bohemond evidently hoped to claim such places without letting go of them later. He recruited warriors to his cause from bases in Italy, and campaigned with some success north of Palestine, around Antioch and Laodicea. But he found himself in trouble with the Emperor for the reason stated. And, evidently being in need of reinforcements and, perhaps, money, he was in a weakened position when he learned of enemy forces approaching.

At this juncture, Bohemond took a desperate expedient, and in a tale which may be true, or may be invented, began a strange plan.

His first move was to float rumors of his own death. Keeping himself hidden, he had a ship prepared to carry home his "remains". A coffin was placed on board and displayed in plain view on deck. In order to sail or row past Byzantine forces and arrive in or near Italy, he would pretend to be dead! The coffin was equipped with air holes and a dead chicken for realistic odors.

Embarking in his coffin, he had the ship depart. He eluded the Byzantines, lying in his coffin whenever the ship made port, and stepping out on deck when the ship was at sea. He reached Corfu safely, and from that island between north Greece and Italy sent defiant, threatening, and blood-thirsty messages to the Byzantines. (This story of Bohemond and his peculiar voyage may be found in *The Alexiad of Anna Comnena*, translated into English by E. R. A. Sewter, Penguin Books, 1985 paperback, pp. 366-368, though Bohemond appears throughout the book in his role of trouble-maker.)

Is it possible that Bohemond made history as the first of the "Undead"? Given adjacent cultures, one wonders if this story may be one basis for folk-tales of the evil creatures that rise from their graves to attack the living.

Vampires as generally presented in folk-lore did not fly or turn to mist or smoke; they did not become bats or command wolves. They appeared to be ordinary persons, even as you or I (see Dudley Wright's *The Book of Vampires*, Dorset Press, New York, 1987). The more exotic attributes, along with a name ("Dracula") reminiscent of a medieval warrior leader of infamous cruelty, were given to the vampire by the British author Bram Stoker. In the old tales, the vampire appears at night walking along the street as any regular inhabitant of the area. A typical person—except that he had died previously.

Given the cruelty of war in the Middle Ages, and the effects of sword, slaughter, and the sack of cities on the general population, invading soldiers might well produce more suffering and bloodshed than dozens of bizarre people that bounced in and out of their tombs.

The Vikings had heard the story of the "coffin-trick". They have a story of the siege of a town that was failing, but which succeeded after a clever Viking ruse. They claimed that their leader had died, but had requested burial in holy ground inside the town. To be buried in a church or in a churchyard was to be buried in "holy" ground in the medieval period, and in the island being attacked, the only church was *inside* the town. The "dead" leader

**17**

# Beasts and Battles

came out of his coffin with his sword in hand after getting inside the walls of the town, and he and his "mourners" engaged in the usual Viking carnage. The Viking version of the story set this scene in the Mediterranean Sea area.

The Byzantines called the soldiers from northwest Europe "barbarians" as well as variously "Franks" or "Latins". And, since the Greek language had gradually supplanted the latin tongue for most purposes in Byzantium (Constantinople) itself, they could refer to themselves as "Greeks' or "Romans" at their preference. They were the heirs to the impressive culture of the past, and could interpose their pious phrases with quotations from Homer and other great pagan figures of earlier times. They also bathed more often than the northerners, though being dirty had come to seem a virtue after the victory of Christianity, as showing a disdain for earthly matters as compared with heavenly things. Still, most peoples of the Byzantine Empire were not hermits or holy men, and the civilization whose heritage they shared provided great public baths. The "Franks" could not quote from Homer, and possessed a somewhat different version of Christianity which was based on the Pope, or Bishop of Rome, and not upon the Byzantine Emperor as both Head of State and Voice of God on Earth.

But the "barbarians" were respected in the sense of being considered dangerous foes with known fighting ability, and the weakened Byzantine Empire had difficulty with them. From his island Bohemond raised troops from Italy, and threatened bloodshed and slaughter across the Adriatic and against Macedonia, Greece, and whatever other area fell into his path. Eventually he found himself again in a weakened military position versus the Byzantines, and at last made peace and went home to Italy after releasing his troops to Byzantine command under fairly favorable terms.

It might be said that, if Bohemond is considered (from the Byzantine viewpoint), as a "vampire", then it was gold and not garlic that conquered him. Byzantium was far wealthier than any single duke or even king of the West—and so could rise from misfortune to triumph later, based on a thriving economy. The coin of Byzantium thus taking the place of garlic, holy water, and wooden stakes, Bohemond was constrained to refrain from more war by a larger and better supplied enemy, and required to depart. After swearing under oath to do and not do certain things, he was allowed to return to Italy, and die in peace. And this time he was really dead and could not again leave his coffin.

As the years passed and the peculiar story of Bohemond spread through Byzantine and adjacent areas, it seems plausible that the legend of the "undead" had begun, if it was not already part of folk beliefs—if such concepts already existed, they may have inspired Bohemond's action and peculiar voyage. We do know that beliefs in dark magic and witchcraft were very ancient as such. Some examples are present in Apuleius' book *The Golden Ass*, though none representing the specific legend of the vampire.

If the story of Bohemond's bizarre escape from danger is an invention, it is nevertheless interesting; it did interest the Vikings, who were ever ready to hear of any clever trick to use against enemies. But the writer of the adventure of the undead warrior presented Bohemond and his coffin as factual in her historical chronicle, the *Alexiad*. She lived from 1083 to 1153 A.D., and was the daughter of the Byzantine Emperor. Bohemond was active before and after 1100 A.D.

Constantinople, in prior ages known as "Byzantium" to the Greeks, the impressive capitol of what we call the Byzantine Empire, lasted for another three hundred years after Anna Comnena died. It managed to survive until 1453 in spite of policies of overtaxation and the attacks of strong new enemies. The combination of canons and Turks finally penetrated the massive walls of the city, and ended the enfeebled city's existence as the last vestige of the Eastern Roman Empire. Today it is called Istanbul.

# ◆ 2 ◀

# BATTLE ODDITY: MARATHON

One of the most intelligent battles ever fought was that of Marathon. It is generally known that the Athenians won that battle by virtue of the way they arranged their formation: they thinned the center of their line and added men to both wings. This brilliant idea won the battle.

The idea just pictured is only half the apparent real story of the battle, though it may have made a contribution to the Athenian victory. There is another important lesson that the battle teaches, but that is never mentioned in regard to the strategy or tactics used. Further analysis shows at least two important elements that must be considered in any view of the situation obtaining at that place in 490 B.C. Before showing these two elements, it may be useful to review the general way that wars were fought in the age of the Battle of Marathon.

The Greeks of the fifth century B.C. had perfected by much use a way of combat that entailed the use of a multiple line of men. These men would be armored in bronze with metal helmets, metal shin-guards and metal breast-plates. They would carry spears and shields, and be armed with swords for close work. When marching the men would be behind each other, though in more than one file depending upon the road followed or the terrain being crossed during the march. When the field of battle was reached, these one-man-behind-another lines would have to re-

# Battle Oddity: Marathon

form in such a way that the men now faced forward side-by-side in lines instead of one-behind-the-other. There would be more than one line, the spears of the second line perhaps protruding horizontally between the men of the first rank, and the spears of those in lines further back perhaps carried with points slanted upward at an angle until the front ranks marched into the mass of the enemy.

One problem with this sort of fighting was that much discipline would be needed to assure success. The lines would march forward together, shoulder to shoulder; the impact of their arrival crashing against the enemy in a solid body would be more effective if all the men moved "as one". The greater the discipline, the greater the shock value of the encounter. Again, if the enemy were suddenly to be met, there would be a great need of discipline to quickly achieve the "in-line-side-by-side" formations, coming out of the "one-man-behind-another" line of march formations. A body of men in line of march would be at a disadvantage, since the bulk of the force might well be a considerable distance behind the leading men. This would be especially true if the march led along narrow roads between hills or mountains. It can be seen that in the event of an ambush, the leading part of the army on the march might well encounter the real danger of being out-numbered and cut up before the rear people could come up—the larger the army, the greater this problem could become, for the rear units might well be spread out for many miles. The ability to quickly form a defensive front might well avert disaster, so again discipline would be vital. Troops would have to be well-drilled and able to execute different formations and changes of direction of march.

Since the Greeks of the fifth century B.C. set much store by ritual, it might be thought that there would always be plenty of time to deploy from line of march into line of battle. Indeed, given the constant wars of the Greek city-states among themselves, it does seem that there must have been some sort of "rules of war" so that the entire land would not lose most of its male population in the various battles. We do know that the Greeks made sacrifices before starting battle, and would frequently refuse to fight (as at the Battle of Plataea), when the sacrifices were "unfavorable" Nevertheless, their fights were not exactly gentlemanly affairs—Herodotus has an account of a fight in which Athenians marching homeward were ambushed by Boeotians (*Persian Wars*,

# Beasts and Battles

Book VI, p. 477 of Random House's Modern Library edition). That the Athenians won that encounter speaks highly of their drill and discipline.

Another need for discipline was the requirement for immediate movement, in formation, to ward off flanking attempts by an opponent. Since the power of the lines in the side-by-side battle-ready formation was directed completely to the front, it might seem that a rear attack would be a problem. This would not be so much a difficulty as it might seem at first, for a rear line or two could lift spears straight up and very quickly turn around. If the first line or two were advancing, it is true that the rear line or two might have to walk backward to avoid creating a gap that the enemy might penetrate; with well-trained troops this should not be a problem. The danger of flanking attacks was a different matter, and one of considerable worry. If the enemy could advance troops around to the side of your formation, he could direct many men in side-by-side ranks against the few men at the far left end or right end of your lines, thus aiming many spears at just a few. This can be seen as just a simple case again of being outnumbered. But the danger would be very serious. The enemy could drive forward in relentless fashion from the end of your line all the way throughout its length (or part of it), throwing the rest of your troops into a turmoil and confusion in which any opponent that remained in their front could attack them now from the side as they turned to meet the danger coming at them from the end of their line. An attack by the opponent starting at the end of your line and slicing forward along its length is what is meant by "rolling up" the flank. This attack could take place against either end of the line, or against both ends at once. The attacked party could attempt to create a box or "L" formation at the command of an officer to prevent the flanking attack succeeding—but here again drill and discipline would be mandatory for the prevention of disaster.

There were weapons in the fifth century B.C. that were effective at a distance: the sling and the bow-and-arrow. The javelin could be thrown. But these devices were little used by major Greek cities in their set-piece battles in the early fifth century. They also had cavalry, but not much of it, and the use of horses was limited due to the rugged mountainous and hilly nature of the terrain in Greece south of Thessaly. Horses might be used for scouting sometimes, and for transportation of supplies by pack-bundle. Horses

# Battle Oddity: Marathon

were ridden without saddles or stirrups, which had yet to be invented. Many scholars have pointed out that the type of harness used in the ancient world prevented horses from pulling much of a load in a cart, because the harness was placed about the neck in such a way that pulling strongly actually choked the horse.

The Persians in the year 490 B.C. decided to punish the Greeks, and especially the Athenians, because of their intervention in what we would today call Persian "internal affairs". The Persians had conquered or received the submission of the Greek cities along the coast of what is now Turkey, but the mainland Greeks had persisted in raids into Asia Minor, and had even raided the capitol of a Persian province, the city of Sardis. Persia ruled a vast territory, including Egypt, Palestine, Mesopotamia, Persia itself (roughly Iran), all the lands from Persia through Pakistan, as well as Asia Minor and some territories recently conquered across the Helles-pont. Persia was the only super-power in the western world, since Alexander the Great was yet to be born, and Roman power was yet to arise.

Darius was Great King of Persia. He relieved of command a general in disfavor, and placed his troops under command of Datis the Mede and Artaphernes, nephew of the Great King. Leaving from Asia Minor, the troops took ship through the Greek islands, raiding which they chose. Some of these islands were parts of the Persian Empire; maybe a part of the fleet that carried Darius' troops were Greek ships, as well as those of the Phoenicians (whose coastal cities were also under Persian domination).

Two cities were the chief targets: Athens and Eretria. Both had sent help to the Greek cities along the coast of Asia Minor and in the off-shore islands which had rebelled against Persian rule; now they were to be punished, and the aged son of a former tyrant to be installed in Athens to keep the Athenians quiet and out of mischief for the future. This man, Hippias, seems to have given some bad advice to the Persian forces at a key moment.

Landing in the island of Euboea to the east of Attica, the country of Athens, the Persians attacked the southern city of Er-etria. After some difficulties the city was betrayed to them, and they burned the temples and made the populace prisoners to take to the Great King later. Having success with half their mission, the troops were now ferried over the intervening water and landed upon the shore of Attica, at the place called the "Plain of Mara-

## Beasts and Battles

thon". They were, according to Herodotus, "conducted" there by Hippias (p. 476), presumably because an open space would favor Persian cavalry. The Persians, unlike the Athenians, used cavalry; it may well have been their best arm, and the resource chiefly responsible for their conquering so vast a territory so quickly (a similarity to the later speed of the Islamic conquests—deriving from the same cause: speed and the advantage of mobility). There is a certain problem with the idea that the Persians landed at Marathon to favor their cavalry, for it seems that their horses were not available during the ensuing battle. Either the cavalry was still in Euboea and was to follow later, or was re-embarked upon the ships at the time of the battle, since it took no part therein. It may be that the Persians wished to avoid a sea-fight with the Athenians, which they could avoid by crossing the narrow body of water separating Euboea from the mainland; then, too, weather may have been a factor. Ancient ships were not able to face storms at sea with any degree of security, and always preferably kept within sight of land. It is also true that to sail to Athens they would have to go a distance south and round a cape. Not only would they face an opposed landing, a great disadvantage in itself, but the fragility of the ancient ships in the event of a storm had caused the Persians a disaster in the previous year, according to Herodotus (p. 471). Weather could make the rounding of a cape of land dangerous, and opposition could only make things worse. But, whatever the reason, the decision to land on the east coast of Attica at Marathon was soon to be seen as a mistake by the Persians.

There was a certain failure to foresee possibilities for the future involved in the landing, which one might suppose the fault of Hippias, the would-be tyrant the Persians intended to establish at Athens. After all, he chose the landing. And as a Greek, he presumably knew the country and the best places to effect an unopposed landing. The area was large enough to not cramp the number of troops, and they could land before the Athenians could arrive to contest the disembarkation.

And it may have seemed that it really did not matter much where they landed, provided that the place was convenient. The power of Persia was feared, and that fear had caused some to counsel surrender to the Great King; there was always a danger of bribery, for Persia was also wealthy beyond belief, and did not hesitate to attempt to purchase friendship among potential ene-

24

## Battle Oddity: Marathon

mies. Cities could be betrayed to the Persians out of greed as well as out of fear. This had happened at Eretria, and the Athenians sent there to help fight the Persians had escaped back to the mainland when warned of how things were (Herodotus, p. 473). Those favoring the Persians among the Greeks were said to be "Medizing". With this in view, it may be that the Persian leaders and Hippias believed that once they had landed safely the Athenians would come to terms and agree to accept the will of the Great King. Indeed, there was a subsequent scandal in which someone among the Greeks had been thought to have signalled the Persians by flashing sunlight off a polished shield in connection with the Persian Marathon expedition (Herodotus, pp. 482-484).

And when the Athenians held a counsel of war to decide what to do, some of the leaders favored compromise and did not wish to fight at all.

It is true that the details of the Battle of Marathon are not available to us except in general terms, as pointed out by J. B. Bury, who noted that these details had become over time confused and partially lost (see his *A History of Greece*, Random House, Modern Library edition, p. 241). Our first historian, Herodotus, writes decades after the events took place.

Nevertheless, some facts remain beyond much doubt: those of the terrain of the plain and nearby areas. This ground contains several lessons which might be drawn from it. The sea level today may be somewhat different, but the low mountains are still there. At the time of the battle there were narrow roads leading away from the plain in more or less southerly and westerly directions, winding between the low mountains. The Greeks could occupy high ground at need, so that cavalry might not be very effective against them; one wonders if that may be why the cavalry was not at the scene—another possible explanation of the missing horse. It would be quite natural for the Greeks to post scouts and light-armed troops on high ground.

The plain itself was divided by a stream, and the northern and southern ends were bordered by marshland. The Persian forces waited on the level ground of the plain; and the Athenian main force which had marched to the area on the news of the Persian landing waited in camp to the northwest and about two miles from the edge of the plain (see map in Bury, p. 238). The Persian fleet remained along the shore.

## Beasts and Battles

The Persians waited, but the Greeks did *nothing whatso-ever*. For whatever the reasons were: divided counsel among the generals as Herodotus wrote, or strategic reasons which have not heretofore been always noticed, the Greeks remained inactive. It is true that they expected help to come from Sparta, and if they waited long enough their forces would be augmented. They had sent to Sparta for aid, but the Spartans would not march before the full moon (not the last time that their religious beliefs affected military matters). It was also true that the Athenians were encamped in a good position. With high ground on either side of a narrow road with limited area to either side, only part of the Persian army at a time could oppose their front, and the enemy could therefore not bring his numerical advantage to bear. They were in effect in the position of a small force holding a narrow pass against a large force, and they could always take high ground if in need of a more defensive posture. Yet they were also close to the Persians.

So the Athenians did nothing, and the Persian army also waited. The Persians could not wait too long, for the Great King would certainly wonder what his army was doing. Doing nothing suited the Greek side, but was not so good for the reputation or the pride of the Persian punitive expedition.

Now the first of the two key elements in the Battle of Marathon may begin to be perceived. *Part of the reason that the battle was won was that the Athenians did nothing for the correct length of time, and at the right place.*

And that brings us to the second important but little-noted reason that the battle was won.

What would happen if the Athenians never offered battle at all? The choices would become unpleasant to the Persian force. It would have to leave. It would have its choice of re-embarking upon the ships or of marching along one of the narrow roads bordered by mountains and high ground.

Throughout all of past history, one of the major aims of an armed force has been to fight the enemy while the enemy is at a disadvantage. Thus if you can outnumber your foe you have a good chance of victory. This may be done by attacking an army when it is crossing a river and only part of its strength has reached your side of the river; if you destroy that portion, your enemy is weaker by the amount of the loss. And easier to defeat. In simple

# Battle Oddity: Marathon

terms, three men should beat one man. There is serious intent behind the old military caution about not dividing one's forces lest they be attacked and beaten piece-meal, a part at a time.

If the Persians re-embarked their forces, the Athenians could attack them in the process—attacking an equal or weaker force instead of facing all the enemy's troops and so being out-numbered. If the Persians advanced along either of the roads leading toward Athens, then they could be attacked in rear and possibly in flank as the leading elements stretched out along the route of march. No ancient commander would want to present the rear of his army to an enemy nearby in the field. No commander would want to have his army straggling along a narrow road, stretched out for miles, while an active enemy could march against his rear.

The second key factor that is sometimes not noticed when the battle is considered is then the result of the first such factor: *if the Athenians do nothing, then the Persians must leave, and in leaving either divide their forces or present their rear to the enemy (again with divided strength).*

They can attack the Athenians in their camp while some of their forces march south toward Athens, but here again they would give the advantage of facing a smaller enemy force to the Athenians. It would seem that the Persians were in a trap. Whatever they did would fail. So may it not be possible that Athenian officers had perceived some of these factors, and that the delay on their part may represent a strategic insight rather than a divided counsel and stalemate among the leaders?

It may be true that this sort of trap would not have damaged the later Romans, who were expert in entrenchments; they could have walled off an area and re-embarked on their ships while some troops defended the walls. The Persians, however, had no experience of trench war-fare. They may have believed the Athenians to be paralyzed by fear and unlikely to move. Whatever they believed, the probabilities are that they finally began to move, and that their movement gave the waiting Athenians their opening to attack in an advantageous situation.

J. B. Bury believed that they began to move their infantry south, and that they had re-embarked their cavalry—his solution to the problem of the missing cavalry (Bury, p. 239). Whatever the actual movement, the time had come to attack.

The Persians did not use the metal body armor of the

# Beasts and Battles

Greeks, but usually carried wicker shields and padded cloth body-armor. They may not have been as well-armed, but they were regular troops and not masses of farmers impressed into service. It is presumed that their military skill was not so high as that of the Greeks, but little is known of their drill or lack thereof.

To prepare the attack, the Athenians did lengthen their line side-wise as is generally well-known; they thinned the center of their line and strengthened both wings (roughly the right and left thirds of the line), by adding men. They then made their infantry attack at a run for at least several reasons, one of which may have been to avoid the effects of Persian archery. It would also have been to their advantage to attack quickly before the Persians could bring more troops into line against them, and take advantage of whatever confusion may have existed in the enemy contingent. The normal method of advance against the opponent was apparently at a steady walk; Herodotus wrote that at the Battle of Marathon the Athenians first introduced the method of advancing upon the enemy at a run (p. 480). Aeschylus the tragic poet fought in the battle (Bury, p. 240). The speed of attack may have surprised the foe.

The Athenian center gave way, but the wings were victorious. One example of the Greek discipline was that both wings joined together to continue the battle against the Persian center, instead of chasing the already defeated remnants of the Persian wings that were desperately fleeing toward their ships. Many times in history, parts of battles have been won but the battle as a whole lost because some force failed to break off pursuit and fight the still dangerous part of the opposing force. The natural tendency is to pursue a foe that runs away instead of confronting a dangerous foe facing one, and one can get caught up in the chase and heat of the moment.

If the thoughts noted above are correct, then we may add to the reasons for victory at Marathon the *clever knowledge that doing nothing would result in the enemy dividing his forces or presenting his rear or flank to attack* to his evident disadvantage. And the presentation of his rear while his leading elements marched away along narrow roads would still be a division of forces, since the lead elements could not quickly turn around on a crowded road and return to a battle in progress.

The real weakness that we have already seen in our brief

# Battle Oddity: Marathon

discussion of the Greek method of fighting at the time would have been the danger of a mass of the enemy getting at the extreme ends of their lines (lines *in toto* were named "phalanx"), and forcing their way down the lines from the side by weight of numbers: the old "rolling up the flank". The flanks or extreme ends of the phalanx on either side were the points of weakness and potential danger to the ancient phalanx. This being the case, we can see at once that the surviving account of the thickening of the sides or wings of the Athenian lines would be likely to be a true memory of the event. The Greeks knew the dangers of enemy flank attack and took what precautions they could against its eventuality. They were "flank happy", so that the tactic of the heavy wings would counter any danger from the flanks in event of trouble there; some of the men at the ends of the lines could turn and face outward if needed. Also, the Athenians had lengthened their lines to spread as widely as the presumed Persian front in order to make attack from the side (flank) more difficult.

Some scholars believe that the tactic of the thickened ends of the phalanx lines was so that when the Persian center pushed back the lighter Greek center line, the heavier Greek wings could push back and destroy the opposing Persian wings, and then close from each side on the advanced Persian center. This may have happened, but from the remaining account in Herodotus (pp. 479-480) it seems that the Persians of the center had chased the (fewer) Greeks in front of them so far that they had almost left the battlefield, and therefore the two victorious Greek wings united and turned and marched against the hitherto victorious Persian center from its rear. The idea of the deep and strong wings of the Greek line had worked well whatever the details of the end of the battle, and this tactic doubtless did play a part in the victory. The victors in ancient battles lost far fewer men than did the vanquished; most of the losses of the latter would occur in the pursuit after the battle had been decided and the losers were running away. With that in mind, the figures Herodotus gives of 192 lost on the Athenian side and 6,400 on the Persian may even be more or less correct. The belief in Persian invincibility was broken and the Greeks able to face their future difficulties with the Persians with more resolution as a result of the battle.

The Persians at Marathon had seemingly put themselves into a problem. The cavalry that was their chief strength was not

# Beasts and Battles

usable in Greece except upon such a plain, so it is easy to see why the Plain of Marathon was chosen as a landing site. If the Greeks offered battle immediatley, the Persians could presumably bring up their cavalry, and the large level plain gave plenty of room for them to muster their numerically much superior army. What they had failed to discern was *the problem that must ensue in the future if the Athenians refused battle initially but attacked later during a Persian attempt at withdrawal.*

It seems likely that the Athenians noted the possibilities inherent in the situation. There may be a slight clue to this in Herodotus' statement (p. 479) that when the Athenian generals finally agreed to attack, and gave some or all command powers to their aggressive general Miltiades, *he did not attack at once, but waited for a number of days.* This is explained by our historian by his belief that Miltiades was waiting for his own later appointed day of command to come about (apparently the generals "took turns"). Yet, based upon the above analysis, may he not have been waiting for the Persians to eventually place themselves at a disadvantage—in keeping with an estimate of the situation arrived at by the Greek commanders? Or was the situation all unplanned coincidence? Since the Greeks of the time were skilled in their type of war-fare (and such skill clearly entailed minimization of casualties), it is possible that the outcome, important for the western world and famous, was the result of careful planning.

Sometimes very simple elements are ignored in the analysis of military situations and potential future situations. There may occur failures due not only to pride and arrogance, but also to factors so simple that they may not be taken into account.

Thus, if one wishes to fight a *defensive war,* there are certain obvious things to consider. Among these are natural advantages of terrain or the lack thereof; can you hold a pass or a bridge against the enemy? Can you hold and defend against attack a narrow neck of land? This last emerged in the later Persian invasion of Greece under Xerxes. The Spartans were determined to barricade the narrow neck of land at the isthmus joining north and south Greece, and fight off the Persian army's advance behind a wall there—until it was pointed out to them that the Persians had access to the Phoenician navy and could sail around their wall and land behind them. In a defensive war it may not always be

## Battle Oddity: Marathon

advisable to occupy what appear to be strong points in the form of fortresses or towns; Machiavelli in his lesser-known book the *Republic* endorsed (probably rightly), the idea of mobile defense throughout a countryside rather than the occupation of towns or forts. Such imagined "strong points" could provide the enemy with points of attack and pin down the defensive forces, whereas an active rather than a static defense might well be more effective. There are exceptions to this—one might name the use of isolated forts in the desert by Alexander the Great, but it may be that he was simply controlling desert water supplies by building forts at various relevant points in a temporary holding action allowed by the terrain. Alexander is famous for mobility, not for forts.

To wage a defensive war in a peninsula should be simple in some ways, provided one has control of the waters on either side. In that case, a defensive line may be drawn across the neck of the peninsula, and the shortness of the defensive line makes possible a defensive strategy that is practical—such as in Korea.

In the case of Vietnam one notices at once the enormous length of the western border of the country. This simple geographical feature would have more to do with strategic difficulties of defense than the many extraneous "reasons" for these problems that one hears usually cited. Clearly there are places where a defensive war is easier to fight. With command of the seas one could defend Florida, for example, by drawing a defensive line across the neck of that peninsula, in which case the general strategic situation would resemble that of Korea. This was not possible in Vietnam due to the nature of border configuration.

An aggressive war to the north across borders in Vietnam would have been a dangerous course at the time of Mao, since one might then have to fight the Chinese; if China were defeated then one might have had to fight Russia—one should stop at this point to reconsider one's options. Asia is endless in many ways, and it might be well to be careful of land wars in Asia, as General MacArthur remarked many years ago. It is not that one cannot fight, but that the nature of the terrain should always be considered.

In Vietnam there were at least two things not under American control: the enormously long western border of the country, and the determination or lack thereof of the North Vietnamese. The latter could only be found out the hard way by testing it, but

## Beasts and Battles

very little could be done about the geographical nature of the border of the country. We see at once the very great difference between defending a peninsula or island and defending a portion of a mainland which extends for a considerable distance down the coast of such mainland. These elements are very simple—perhaps too simple to be noticed, but it is such factors that impinge directly and to a great degree upon one's strategic position and may lead to great, if not insuperable, difficulties. No matter what claims or posture on "planning" might be held, the fixed geographical facts of Vietnam would not change, and would always be a constant and unchangeable factor of difficulty and problem.

It was possible that technology could counter-balance the elements of geographical difficulty and "will of the enemy", and that a defense of South Vietnam could be made successful by virtue of technological superiority; this could not be known until it was attempted.

The importance of geographical features in military history may clearly be seen in the Battle of Marathon, and in the later Vietnam War. While we may not be condemned to repeat the past because of lack of knowledge of it (as the modern philosopher Santayana said), it is probably true that the future will resemble the past (as the much earlier Thucydides wrote), and we should therefore take cognizance of the details of events of the past in order to learn from them. Such details sometimes contain surprising logical elements.

# ▶ 3 ◀

# PUZZLES OF CYRUS THE GREAT AND HANNIBAL

Cyrus, now Great King of Persia and the Persian Empire which he had created, was campaigning northward in order to extend his borders and enlarge his empire. According to our old friend Herodotus, whose *Persian Wars* represent the western world's earliest surviving history, his aim was to conquer yet another people. These were the "Massagetae", thought by our historian to be "Scythians". Scythians were in general horse nomads that wandered the steppes north of the Black Sea; but this tribe lived north of the Araxes River, south of the Caucasus Mountains, and west of the Caspian Sea. The river Araxes (the modern Araks), trends in a west-to-east direction. It flows from its headwaters in the general area of the beginnings of the Euphrates River, and enters the western side of the Caspian Sea. This river seems to have been the southern boundary of what Herodotus believed to be the Massagetae "kingdom", and it also represents the northern border of the Persian kingdom. East of the Caspian Sea and fading away into the distance was a vast plain, which Herodotus noted as belonging to the same Massagetae. This plain (more or less in the position of the modern Turkmen S.S.R. of the southern Soviet Union), seems more suited to the use of a horse nomad people of considerable size than does the smaller area boxed in by mountains, Araxes River, and Caspian Sea. Indeed, since the Araxes enters the Caspian Sea more than a hundred miles north of that

# Beasts and Battles

Sea's southern end, the Massagetae would have to cross Persian territory to reach the great eastern plain by circling the south end of the Sea. Unless the Massagetae habitually crossed the Caspian Sea by boat—unlikely for a nomad people moving as a tribe—then the only other way to reach the great distant plain that they "possessed" would have been to cross the Caucasus Mountains and circle around the north end of the Caspian Sea. That is possible, but another belief of Herodotus seems to confuse the account: he believed that the west side of the Caspian Sea was bordered by the Caucasus Mountains, described as very high and extensive.

Many writers have pointed out how Herodotus' descriptions become more doubtful the further from the Mediterranean the phenomena described. The wording of the text (Book I, Ch. 204), seems to indicate that he thought that the Araxes River was to be found to the east of the Caspian Sea (where the great plain possessed by the Massagetae was located), instead of to the west of that Sea where modern knowledge places it. Or it may be that the Araxes was not the river in question, and that Cyrus was campaigning northward *to the east* of the Caspian Sea and not northward west of it. These confusions arise when following Herodotus' account in conjunction with geographical information contained in modern maps.

The exact location of the events in the accounts (if they really took place), would be interesting, but is not vital to the logical question posed in this discussion. For our purposes, we shall leave the "kingdom" of the Massagetae in the area more or less occupied by the Azerbaijan S.S.R. of the Soviet Union, north of the Araxes (Araks) River, west of the Caspian Sea, and south of the Caucasus Mountains, with hilly country and rugged terrain to its west. We will not hold Herodotus responsible for fifth century B.C. geographical ignorance; the puzzle of the placement of the Massagetae on the map is not the particular puzzle of our interest here.

Horse nomads in the normal course of things did not have kingdoms as such, but rather vast areas of potential pasture in which to move constantly from place to place for new grazing. For a numerous tribe of nomads, amazing amounts of space would be required. It would be easy for such nomads to prevent attack by enemies through the simple method of moving away and keeping at a distance from pursuing forces. The first problem would be to locate them, and this could not be done unless they willed

34

# Puzzles of Cyrus the Great and Hannibal

it so, or unless they were pursued by other nomads or equally mobile cavalry. And their ability to use archery at a distance made them especially dangerous opponents.

Centuries after Cyrus's adventures at Herodotus' Araxes River, Roman legions under Crassus suffered a disastrous defeat by the Parthians—a people using cavalry as a main weapon of war, though perhaps more sophisticated than the earlier horse nomads. Parthians, who supplanted Persia as a power in later centuries, used body armor for their mounted warriors as well as on the horses to a certain extent, but the major difficulty of foot soldiers in facing mounted enemies would always be chiefly the problem of coming to close combat with them. Cavalry using bow and arrow from a distance would be a dangerous and frustrating opponent; the taking of casualties without the ability to respond or inflict any hurt to the enemy could destroy an army. It was against the Parthians that Julius Caesar evidently planned to campaign when his death intervened and prevented the expedition.

Only generals of talent could combat a mounted enemy army. The Roman legions, invincible when properly led against foot soldiers like themselves, had terrible experiences with Hannibal's army before Caesar's time, and suffered badly until they learned how to deal with an enemy that used a high proportion of mounted troops (the Romans themselves used cavalry only for scouting, couriers, and sudden charges against the enemy to confuse the opposing troops—cavalry only represented about 5% of a typical Roman force: roughly 6,000-odd foot and 300 cavalry).

Horse nomads or any ancient mounted enemy could inflict wounds and death from a distance by simply riding around an opposing army and discharging their weapons at long range. When the army suffering under their attacks rushed out at them, they could always retreat, keep at a distance, and then return later to again discharge their weapons. An army on foot had no chance of defeating these tactics. It could save itself by finding a walled city to occupy, or by marching away in retreat while using its own archers and slingers to keep the enemy cavalry at a distance.

The Greek Xenophon and his ten thousand men escaped from Mesopotamia despite pursuit by mounted Persian cavalry thorugh use of their own missile troops to keep the Persians at a distance, and the obtaining of horses of their own when possible. Julius Caesar may once have fought his way out of trouble with

# Beasts and Battles

cavalry by forming a circle that moved steadily in retreat toward safety while periodically sending a small force of cavalry and light-armed foot in charges from inside his defensive perimeter. Such charges, amusingly similar to sudden sallies from a town or fort under siege, would serve to drive off the circling enemy temporarily—long enough for the whole formation to march awhile in retreat and gain some distance toward the safety of a town or fortified place. When the enemy returned in force against the small foray, that little force could retreat back inside the protection of the defensive perimeter, while the whole formation could halt at need to repel any too close enemy attack—and repeat the same maneuvers time after time until the army reached safety.

Even in the time of Alexander the Great, his army was not wholly cavalry, though cavalry may have been important to basic tactics in his battles. He once achieved success against horse nomads by preparing two mounted spearheads for sudden attack; these, bursting from his forces towards the mounted nomads then using their typical encircling tactic, cut off a segment of their cavalry between the spearheads and destroyed the horsemen so trapped (recounted in General Fuller's *Generalship of Alexander the Great*). In a later age, the Roman general Scipio had learned to deal with an enemy army equipped with cavalry, and by defeating Hannibal of Carthage in Africa had earned the name of Scipio "Africanus". But many commanders lacking the requisite talent or genius of Alexander, Scipio, or Julius Caesar came to grief at the hands of nomads who were wholly mounted and fought with the simple tactic of "riding around" their enemy and using the bow and arrow.

Even the impressively armored knights of the European medieval period could not deal with the nomad warriors of Genghis Khan. It almost seems unfair that these heavily armored men could not "catch" and come to close grips with the Mongols during the battles of their European invasion. The lighter boiled leather or quilted cloth armor of a nomad might be weaker than heavy metal armor, but a knight weighed down by his armor could be destroyed by killing his horse from a distance and using arrows or looped ropes to finish the job. Whatever the exact method employed by the mongols, the result was that mobility (and perhaps cooperative discipline) won and defeated slow and armored strength. In a certain sense this repeats the result of one of the first appearances of heavy body armor in Europe: in his book on his war in Gaul (modern France), Caesar mentions an early attempt at heavy body armor by the Gauls. Some of their infantry were encased in heavy metal armor, so that the Roman soldiers could make no impression upon them by javelin or sword. But this auspicious beginning soon came to nothing, as the Romans found that they could incapacitate such armored figures by using branches or saplings to push them over backwards. Once down, these early walking forts were helpless.

An ancient commander could take various precautions to protect his foot soldiers from attack by cavalry. A method not already mentioned would be occupation of high ground, since cavalry operates best on the level plain and does not charge up steep slopes effectively; it also cannot work well in rugged terrain, which limits its possibilities of encirclement and attack against the enemy rear or flanks. Trenches or pits to disable charging units might be effective, or encampment behind the stone walls of a town. But any strategy of defense that entailed the occupation of a particular place for any length of time would be limited by the need for food and water for the defensive force. A woodland might provide good shelter from enemy cavalry and from their missiles as well, but might not provide sufficient food or water. Julius Caesar's legions in Gaul used metal spiked devices to disable horses' feet, and earth entrenchments and wooden encampment walls, but the Roman armies always had more technical ability than many other historical forces.

A direct charge by enemy cavalry against foot soldiers could always be met effectively by the use of spears with their butt ends braced against the ground, and their sharp points slanted upward and outwards against the enemy horse. Perhaps for that reason, and the possible fear of concealed pits or trenches, nomads have often adopted the practice in war already noted of "riding around" an enemy and firing missiles from a distance. The American Indians used this tactic, and the wagon trains they attacked used the "circle" formation that Caesar may have made; one tactic used through the ages by a small force when attacked by a large force has always been to "make a circle" or "form a square" and face outwards in all directions.

The simplest way in which an ancient commander could deal with enemy cavalry effectively would seem to be to get cavalry

# Beasts and Battles

for his forces in number sufficient to engage the opponent's cavalry with his own. This may have been what Scipio Africanus had learned to do, and may (or may not) have been what Julius Caesar intended to do in his projected plans to fight the Parthian horsemen that destroyed Crassus and his army. Later the Roman Emperor Julian came to grief against a similarly located power, and since he was campaigning in Mesopotamia (and Mesopotamian terrain is flat and level and therefore suitable for the effective use of cavalry), one suspects that once again the ancient difficulty of the foot soldier attempting to fight the mounted warrior had intruded upon history. One had to know what one was doing in contending with horsemen, and ancient battlefields were littered with the bones of those without such knowledge or ability.

If the difficulty of an ancient army in dealing with mounted nomads is our first historical puzzle in connection with the advance of Cyrus the Great to the Araxes River, our second puzzle is identical to the one presented to Cyrus in Herodotus' record. Cyrus had come to the northern limit of his own kingdom or controlled territory, and had decided to cross the river and advance into the next northern territory, adding the land of the "Massagetae" to his empire. For this he began to have bridges constructed for the crossing. He was interrupted by a puzzling message from the queen of the Massagetae.

This message began by stating that peace was better than war. The puzzling part was the offer that followed. Cyrus was given the choice (if he was determined on war), between two courses of action. He could retreat three days' march and allow the Massagetae to cross the river, and then they could fight; otherwise, the Massagetae would retreat three days' march and allow Cyrus and the Persians to cross—and again, a battle could be fought.

Cyrus' generals unanimously agreed that they themselves should fall back and allow the Massagetae to cross. Cyrus then was given an alternate opinion by a famous king, a man he had made captive in a former war and now apparently taken into his service: Croesus, the legendary king of immense wealth. Croesus began by cautioning that fortune in human affairs can be changeable: one must take the possibility of loss of a battle into account. This was quite true, of course, but dangerous to say to a Persian Great King, most of whom seem to have preferred flattery. Croesus then made his point: if the battle was lost on Cyrus' side of the

# Puzzles of Cyrus the Great and Hannibal

river, all his kingdom would be open at once to be captured by the enemy; but if he crossed the river and won the battle, the Massagetae "kingdom" would fall to him immediately. This advice was capped with the fatal argument that it was against Cyrus' dignity to retreat before a foe.

Because of the breadth and relative speed of Cyrus' conquests, it is likely that cavalry made up a considerable part of his army. And since the Persian education was based on learning to "use the bow and tell the truth", it is probable that the Persians could match Massagetae archers with bowmen of their own. In considering the puzzle presented by the question of "who should cross the river?", we might consider the elements of horse mobility and archery ability to be relatively even between the two opposing peoples. We have no information on the relative sizes of the armies, and are not sure of the absolute historical correctness of the story Herodotus gives. Nevertheless, we will accept the scene that he presents, and will attempt to solve the puzzle of deciding the river crossing.

We know that one classic way of winning a battle is to attack a smaller force with a larger. If one side attempts to cross a river, it could be defeated by being attacked in mid-crossing; but the terms of retreat from the river for three days' marching disance should prevent that from happening. With the land being fairly flat it is not likely that a concealed ambush could take place. And the side advancing to cross the river would doubtless send forward scouts to be sure that the enemy was not in the vicinity.

With the scene as presented here, what should Cyrus decide?

What would the reader do?

For purposes of discussing the puzzle, we will presume that a retreat of three days' march for either side would not present either with a problem of finding sufficient water. It may be that springs or side-streams to the river in question were present, but we will consider that water was plentiful for purposes of discussion (although it is true that if we are three days away from the river, marching in retreat, then the army would be six days away from water). But we will postulate that food or water supply problems do not enter into the question at hand.

Cyrus decided that he should cross the river. In the event,

# Beasts and Battles

he preferred Croesus' arguments and crossed the river and advanced with dignity and pride unimpaired. Was he right?

Subsequent happenings do not prove the decision one way or the other. Cyrus and his Persians could have won or lost a battle on either side of the river. The story goes that the Persians defeated part of their foe by use of treachery and a banquet, and in a later battle were defeated by the Massagetae. (Persians were generally believed to use treachery at meetings, and in fact seem to have done so about two hundred years later when they murdered leaders of a Greek army with which Xenophon travelled; his *Anabasis* gives the details.)

Cyrus was killed in the battle. The queen of the Massagetae had a skin filled with blood from the corpses of the battlefield and had the head of Cyrus' body stuffed into the liquid, giving him his fill of blood. This gory touch seems to be doubtful, since Cyrus was placed in a masonry tomb in Persia, making it seem as though the Persians probably retained his body.

From a strictly military point of view, what are the key logical things to consider in deciding whether to advance and cross the Araxes River or to allow the enemy army to do so? Some people believe that pride and morale are all-important, but that can be a misleading element if not used properly. Others believe that one should "never retreat"; but that can be the height of stupidity on occasion, and in any event unduly limits one's mobility and choice of action.

One might say that the military art consists in minimizing one's own casualties while inflicting maximum casualties upon the enemy. With that precept in mind, one can see at once that *Cyrus should have retreated and allowed the Massagetae to cross the river.* The reasons are quite simple.

The choice seems the correct one whether the ensuing fight is won or lost. If the Persians won, the defeated Massagetae might be trapped with their backs to the river and lose a great number of warriors unable to escape; if the Persians lost, they could save more of their troops by flight if not blocked by a river at their back. If the Persians crossed the river, these factors are reversed, and would turn to the advantage of the Massagetae.

Finally, Croesus' argument about "kingdoms" being overrun seems to be nonsense and very superficial. For one thing, nomad horsemen do not have "kingdoms" in the usual sense, but simply grasslands over which they wander; there may be no strong points or cities to occupy. One does not "capture" a large grassland plain. For another thing, if the river was easy to cross in order to give battle, it would also be easy to cross in either direction after a battle was won.

Infantry would be much more affected by having a river at their back after a loss than would cavalry; but even cavalry would be affected to some degree, and sustain losses as men in panic flight and confusion—some with wounded horses—attempted to force their way into and across a river with the victorious enemy cutting men down at the edge of the group. The arguments put into Croesus' mouth, whatever their source, seem so far from simple military logic that it leads one to wonder if Croesus in the account might wish Cyrus to be destroyed.

While it is often necessary in aggressive war to advance against the opponent, one should not refuse a "gift" from the enemy which results in their putting their own forces at a disadvantage. *Opposing forces should be allowed to make mistakes.* Thus the Athenians gathered near the edge of the field of Marathon did not attack the Persian expeditionary force at once, although their function was to defend Athens and stop the Persian advance. Seeing that the Persians must leave the Plain of Marathon by re-embarkation of their troops or by marching their troops away along narrow roads between mountains (thus presenting a rear to the Greeks, and a rear not in battle formation at that), the Athenian forces *allowed the Persians to make the mistake of dividing their forces.*

It is true that generally an active and aggressive policy is far preferable to a defensive mentality in military pursuits. And it is also true that there are very few occasions in which doing nothing is the best policy, (as when the Athenians at Marathon refused for many days to do battle with the Persians at a place and time of the Persians' choosing). Yet it is also true that the recognition of the possibilities of advantage in given situations can be of utmost importance, and that the perception of very simple factors can sometimes be of great value. The Battle of Marathon took place approximately thirty years after the death of Cyrus, and in that time men had not suddenly acquired vast military knowledge. And Cyrus the Great clearly was not an incapable battle leader.

Perhaps the difference is one of arrogance. It might well be

# Beasts and Battles

remembered that, whereas the Persian kings enjoyed being flattered and having their opinions praised and accepted, the later Romans had a practice the purpose of which was to attempt to subdue arrogance or haughty pride. As their conquering generals rode along in celebration of their "Triumphs", a man standing behind them cautioned them to remember that they "were mortal", repeating the phrase in order to off-set the cheers of the crowd and the majesty of the moment.

In the modern world the rational aims of war seem to have been forgotten, perhaps because of the development of air power and later missile armaments. The ancient idea of defeating the enemy's field army and capturing his cities for taxation of them seems to have been lost.

The concept of "total war" seems especially peculiar when history suggests that yesterday's enemy may be tomorrow's ally, and yesterday's ally tomorrow's foe. The ideas of making war on civilians and "teaching them a lesson" and "breaking their morale" simply becomes a cover for extending war beyond its rational purposes and releasing the hatred of the enemy (that is a natural part of all wars). It may be true that aerial weapons can counter-balance vast conventional ground forces, but it then seems more reasonable in principle to attempt to target those very ground forces instead of civilian populations. (The arguments against making war on civilian populations are well made by the British General Fuller in his book *The Generalship of Alexander the Great.*)

The enemy's volunteering to put itself at Cyrus' disposal in his Araxes River campaign was an offer which limited their mobility, and Cyrus was correct to accept it if he remained determined to fight. Other Persian Great Kings were completely unable to catch up with Scythian nomads and bring them to battle.

But the decision to cross the river was an error because of the predictable tactical situation resulting during the aftermath of battle which was either won or lost. Crossing or not crossing would not help to win or avoid loss, but the possible use of the river as a barrier blocking retreat should have been more closely examined.

Wisdom does not always consist in immediately confronting a stronger enemy advancing against your forces; sometimes one must "bide one's time". The Russians in the early nineteenth

# Puzzles of Cyrus the Great and Hannibal

century retiring before Napoleon were correct. The Romans, having suffered disastrous defeats in facing Hannibal of Carthage more than once in his invasion of Italy, finally produced a general who decided to keep the Roman army on high ground and avoid a direct pitched battle. Until the Romans found ways to deal with Hannibal's cavalry and tactics, this was a good idea. An intact Roman army that remained in the advantage of high ground and yet followed Hannibal's army would constrain Hannibal's choices of action, and the future might present some unexpected advantage and opening for attack. This state of affairs ended when another Roman general took his turn at command and decided that courage and action was a better idea. When he ordered the attack, his army was again defeated, and Hannibal regained complete freedom of action.

Scholars have often wondered why Hannibal did not march directly on Rome after one of his victories in the field. While the answer may never be known, it may be that a political motive could produce a key to the puzzle. Some scholars have speculated that Hannibal hoped that Rome's allies in Italy would drop away from her at the defeat of her field armies. They might be expected to at least declare neutrality, if not to come over to the side of the successful Carthaginians. In that event Rome would be isolated. If we combine that idea with the failure to march on Rome at once, we see that Hannibal could have been waiting to allow news of his victories to spread, with the delay allowing the hoped-for political events to happen. Early on, Rome was just a city among cities, and many of her allies had been defeated by her in battle, to become allies later on. If these allies defected, Hannibal could march and lay siege to a weakened and isolated Rome without having to worry about being attacked in his rear by those allies.

Historians sometimes remark that Hannibal made the wrong decision. The allies remained loyal for the most part, and Hannibal "lost" his chance to take the city he seems to have hated—and Rome eventually won the war.

But Hannibal's choice not to march on Rome was not an obvious error. It may have been based on reasonable suppositions, if the political aim mentioned is correct. If the future developed in a different way than expected, it is true that such often happens. And winners of battles with the Romans in this era often took considerable casualties themselves; it may be that Hannibal

# Beasts and Battles

thought his army now too weak to mount a successful siege. As a marauder in a foreign land, he also may have had to pause to allow his army to forage for food.

Hannibal had certainly not evaded one of the chief aims of war: he had not failed to fight and defeat the enemy field army. In fact, he had done this numerous times. We do not know whether there were real difficulties that prevented him from following up his victories. Given his success as a general commanding battles, we probably cannot judge his conduct at all, and his specific choice of action at any one juncture must remain a mystery to us.

Hannibal's enemies had a rather different problem, which concerned how to pin Hannibal down so that he could be defeated in a crushing and conclusive way. Hannibal was obviously a wily tactician with a good capacity for movement. He could be defeated and yet recover and fight again, just as the Romans had done. To trap him might be difficult. Scipio of Rome found the key. He forced Hannibal to come to meet him. Hannibal no longer had the choice of ravaging Italy, for Scipio landed in Africa and menaced the city of Carthage itself. He had found the "Wasp-nest", and the "wasps" had to stop stinging abroad and return to North Africa to defend their home. The mobility of the Carthaginian army was thus neutralized. If Hannibal lost a battle near his home city, the war would effectively be ended; if he and the remnant of his defeated forces took flight in order to stay active, the Romans could simply have taken and destroyed the Carthaginian home. This alternative being unacceptable, Carthage would make peace on Scipio's terms, and would force Hannibal to do so as well. The Roman plan succeeded, and Scipio won and ended the war by defeating one of the great generals known to history, and clearly one of the boldest and most energetic.

This very boldness and energy leads one to believe that some real cause must have prevented Hannibal from beseiging and capturing Rome. The general who planned to campaign in Italy by using a march from Spain, through France, and over the Alps with elephants, was hardly a general lacking the energy or imagination to march along a road and capture a city. He may have been ill. But whether the cause was illness, casualties among his men, misjudgment of the size of the enemy facing him (Italy was far more populous than Carthaginian North Africa), lack of food, or some other reason, we do not know. Since much of his army was composed of mercenaries, it may be that he faced mutinous behavior by mercenaries that squabbled over booty taken from the fallen foe, or demanded their pay. It may be that he needed to replace horses lost through battle (since cavalry was one of his advantages over the Romans). It may be that he had to wait for reinforcements on the march to join him, or for pay for the troops to arrive from Carthage.

The result must be that we cannot judge Hannibal's conduct, and, since his impact upon history demonstrated a talent for generalship of a formidable nature, we must give him the benefit of the doubt and admit that there is much that will forever remain obscure. As Rome could lose, and lose, and rise to fight yet again,—so Carthage could lose, and lose, and use its wealth to hire more mercenaries and rise to fight again. That Scipio interrupted this process and ended the war leads us to respect his planning; and his defeat of Hannibal leads us to hold him in yet higher regard.

# ▶ 4 ◀

# WAS SIR LANCELOT REAL?

The English writer Robin Lane Fox made a good case for a real historical character making an effort to emulate an imaginary character, or at least a legendary (and perhaps semi-imaginary) character. He contended that Alexander the Great was so impressed by the stories of Achilles that he strove to copy the attributes of Achilles. He would use him as the pattern of his own acts. If one reads of Alexander's career, it would seem that Fox was correct in this judgment. Alexander was brave even to a foolhardy extent; he always led his troops in the cavalry charges that decided most of his battles. As Achilles was the "best" fighting man on the Achaian side in the Trojan War, so Alexander continually made efforts to be in the forefront of action. When his troops gave him trouble he remembered the story of Achilles and "sulked in his tent" away from them until they came around to agreement with him, or until it became plain that they never would do so.

The idea of guiding one's conduct through the copying of great examples is nothing new—some might even say that it represents a good educational tool.

It is somewhat rarer that a real historical person might inspire an imaginary character. Even in the early times of the keeping of records and the singing of the songs of the heroes and leaders of the day, the real character at the base of the story might quickly become over-laid with more and more new and fabulous qualities and adventures. Thus Theodoric, the leader that set up an Ostrogothic kingdom in Italy becomes almost unrecognizable

**46**

# Was Sir Lancelot Real?

in the "Dietrich" stories. And it is not yet clear whether or not the British "King Arthur" figure is completely fictional or not. Charlemagne represents himself in the ancient literature, though the picture is not necessarily true to life.

With these things in mind, it becomes clear that in some sense it is true that literary characters can hardly ever be reduced to a portrait of a real historical personage. We naturally have to take account of "artistic license"; or, as Thucydides described it near the end of Chapter One (Book I, *Pelopponesian War*): poetic "exaggeration". And some literary characters are certainly completely fictional.

There are cases in which real historical people are portrayed in a (more or less) realistic way in literature; the Icelandic Sagas may be a case in point.

Finally, one wonders if there may be yet another category in which a real person inspires a fictional character *of another name entirely*. There are certainly a number of similarities in the stories of "Sir Lancelot" and a certain medieval Englishman.

Did "Sir Lancelot" die in 1219 A.D.? He had not somehow added an extra seven hundred years to his age, though it seems true that the tales of King Arthur point to times as long ago as 500 A.D. The "Lancelot" that may have died in 1219 was not the original at all; his virtues and attributes may have been noted and may well have been transposed back upon a figure in the tales of Arthur and his knights—placed in a previous time. It may even be that the man who died in the 13th century was the cause of "Lancelot" being invented by the tellers of tales and medieval writers.

There was no Lancelot (or "Launcelot", if you prefer), in the early writings about King Arthur. Geoffrey of Monmouth, writing before the mid twelfth century (perhaps in 1136 A.D.[1]), has no mention of a Lancelot at all.

Lancelot was among the figures around Arthur that had no early British (Welsh) counterparts[2]—figures added by French and German writers. A Lancelot appears in the works of Chrétien de Troyes, a partially described figure compared with his full-blown portrait in Malory's *Morte D'Arthur* later. Chrétien de Troyes wrote sometime from 1170 to 1190 A.D.[3] The Burgundian knight Robert de Boron, active after 1190 A.D.,[4] is given credit by the Arthurian scholar Richard Barber for the idea of extending Arthurian romances into a larger scale[5]; after him unknown authors created an enlarged cycle of stories.[6] Some scholars place the emergence of French tales about Lancelot in the years 1225-1230 A.D.[7] In any event, when Caxton published Malory's *Morte D'Arthur* in 1485 A.D., Lancelot had replaced Gawain as the chief hero.[8] The dates here given are the important things. Could a man who died in 1219 A.D. as "an old man" be a person that inspired a literary figure that entered history at the times (roughly) cited? In Malory's Lancelot we have a figure fully presented in all his completeness of intimidating strength and unfortunate weakness; he has a "fatal flaw"—in his case affecting his love life.

The man who may have been Lancelot's model seems to have had no such flaw (though he was accused of it), and indeed seems almost too strong, heroic, loyal, and perfect to be true. This man was the lowly-born (at least non-noble) William Marshal, who died in May of 1219. In our day he is almost unknown, though in truth a real English hero of the stature of Nelson or even Marlborough. He is almost forgotten in our day—very little-known; we prefer to go to the romances or films for our knightly heroes.

The date of William's birth is not known, for records of all happenings were not kept during the Middle Ages, and so an obvious question to ask is: how "old" is "old"? In the medieval period people did not live so long as we do in the modern world; in some sense, then, a person in his fifties would be "old" in terms of average life expectancy of the age. Yet the dates do seem to fit. The famous incident wherein William challenged and unhorsed Richard Lionheart seems to have taken place in 1189 A.D., the year of the death of Richard's father, Henry II.[9] From then it is thirty years until William Marshal died as "an old man". But how could a French figure—Lancelot—become an English hero? Some historians see Richard Lionheart as more French than English, yet he made such a transition easily.

After King John died in 1216, William led the English forces in battle to repel the French. He was victorious at the Battle of Lincoln, and in that finale saved England from the political result of a sort of "Agincourt in reverse"; when the French prince was repulsed, England would not become even temporarily part of a potential French empire. William was Regent then (as well as Earl of Pembroke), a reward for a lifetime of loyal service to successive kings, beginning with Henry II and concluding with King John's small son. And with it all he was, of course, a knight.

# Was Sir Lancelot Real?

Lancelot had his castle ("Joyous Gard"), and William had his (perhaps more than one). Lancelot had domains "overseas", and so had William. William held lands in France, and also some lands "overseas" that lay in another direction: in Ireland. (At the time of Magna Carta there had been a "Marshall" coat-of-arms divided gold-and-green behind the rampant lion.)

Lancelot in the stories is French; William Marshall was English—as shown in Georges Duby's excellent book *William Marshal, The Flower of Chivalry* (pp. 3, 14). But the Norman court was more French than English—they spoke French, and French was their culture. Further, to preserve some of his holdings in France, William had sworn fealty to the French king to safeguard his ownership of them (but was vassal just for them, and not "in toto"). These things do not make William French, but they do show how easy it was for the French "troubadors" to have access to his quality and achievements—he who had become Earl and Regent of England by virtue of his own talents, strength, character, and knightly prowess (and not by reason of birth).

The English war with France had gone badly in King John's reign, and it was not unreasonable that the French king would appropriate William's continental holdings had he not sworn some fealty for them. But insuring his ownership of lands across the Channel caused trouble with King John, to whom he owed more direct and complete feudal service; such divided loyalty would prevent William engaging in aggressive war against the French king (Duby, pp. 141-143). In this trouble he nevertheless escaped the worst of King John's anger because none of the sovereign's followers dared to face him in the ritual fight of "trial by combat".

Even in his old age, William Marshal was a formidable fighting man; no knight wished even then to face him in single combat. If the older knights would avoid facing him because of respect, the younger knights and those who hung about the king were daunted by his reputation. Like Lancelot he was invincible in fighting. He was never defeated in battle in the tournaments so much a part of the knightly world of that day. In the melees of teams of knights, his team always won. He had even faced down Richard Lionheart and killed his horse while sparing Richard's life, an event described in Gillingham's *Richard the Lionheart*.[10]

The incident with Richard had occurred while Richard was making war on his father, Henry II—in whose service William was at the time. This tragic war of son-against-father was apparently caused by a power dilemma in which Henry II was caught: he would like to be an emperor with kings under his command, and to do this he would have to make his sons kings of different lands. But if he made his sons kings, he would lose all power of command; if he did not make them kings, the delay would anger them into enmity with him—and his wars with France complicated the entire picture.

The service in defense of Henry II had not prevented Richard taking William Marshal into his own service upon his father's death; indeed, he enriched him with an heiress and lands of considerable extent (Gillingham, p. 125). For William was known to be absolutely loyal to whomsoever he served.

Lancelot saved the life of Arthur's queen. William saved the French prince from capture and ransom after the French defeat at Lincoln, and possibly from accidental harm to his body. Although William at the time was an old man, he personally escorted the prince to the coast and safety (a "chivalric" gesture especially appreciated in France).

Lancelot may have seduced a queen. Oddly enough, William Marshal was rumored to have done this. In William's case, the queen was Margaret, wife of a son Henry of Henry II, whose service William had to leave over this affair. She was daughter of a king, and sister of a future king of France (cf. Duby, pp. 47-48); the affair is presented as a plot to harm William. This does seem to reflect closely the literary scene of "Lancelot discovered with the Queen". Could it be the other way around? Could William's trouble, caused by jealous rivals, have served as a literary model? In any case, William denied the charge, and none would then face him in "trial by combat" over the issue. He left that employ over the thing, only to be taken back later.

At the end of his career, Sir Lancelot became a monk or hermit. And so did William Marshal. Shortly before he died, William joined the Templars in fulfillment of an old vow (cf. Duby, p. 15). The Templars were monks of a war-like sort, and not allowed to have wives. A curious parallel.

Lancelot in Malory's work is shown more than once to be the best or strongest of the knights.[11] Such a description is echoed in the praises spoken by the French king on hearing of William Marshal's death (Duby, pp. 25-26). Or did these praises antedate

# Was Sir Lancelot Real?

those of the literary knight? Duby, in his fine book on William, calls him a "perfect knight" (p. 45). (To be fair to that author, it should be noted that the idea that William "preceded" Lancelot or "parts" of him is not in his book.)

Throughout the wars of English kings he served, William was used as ambassador in talks with the French when diplomacy was needed—his knightly prowess and loyalty was evidently tempered with some wisdom, or at least with common sense.

He lived a long time, especially considering the medieval life expectancy, and in May of 1219 A.D. he died—a great and stately figure; a true hero almost forgotten by our age. A man who left deep impressions on the people of his times. He may well have inspired the literary figure of Lancelot, or at least fleshed out such a figure with famous attributes loaned from reality.

# ▶ 5 ◀

# PUZZLES OF ALEXANDER THE GREAT

Not the least of the puzzles about Alexander the Great consists in his overall success and lack of failure in all of his sieges and battles. There are, however, some other questions, some of which will always be unclear.

There are, firstly, puzzles that have been raised by some scholars, only to be solved by others. Such are the "puzzles of delay"; in a general famous for speed and mobility, there were times when Alexander seemed to wait an unduly long time for no particular reason. One such time is his wait in the already conquered area of Phoenician Tyre, before marching inland to face Darius' huge army. One possible solution to that delay is that Darius had to be given time to raise his army for the confrontation, so that Alexander would not have to chase him through unfriendly territory, encountering possible supply problems. A final conclusive battle would obviate a chase. (This idea is found in Robin Lane Fox, *Alexander the Great*, Dial Press, 1973, pp. 222-223.) A second time of potential "delay" was at Persepolis, the captured Persian capitol. The correct answer has very likely been supplied by two good reasons: lack of food supplies, and the winter climate that blocked the mountain passes to the north with snow and ice until late spring or even summer; (reasons provided by Donald W. Engels in his *Alexander the Great and the Logistics of the Macedonian Army*, University of California Press, 1980 paperback, pp. 73-78; his book is a very useful study of supply problems).

# Puzzles of Alexander the Great

But there are other questions to consider. One might ask whether the early histories of Alexander omit or play down any set-backs he may have been involved with in a personal manner; political motives as well as flattery to Alexander might be thought to justify such recounting of successes. This may not be so, since such histories did include unfortunate events such as his drunken murder of his companion Cleitus. And one must allow for the hatred of the subjugated Athenians when they wrote about Alexander; their complete freedom of action had been taken from them by Alexander and his father Philip.

Other puzzles remain. Why did Alexander attack the fort of Gaza, held by men loyal to Darius, when Egypt was ready to fall with almost no effort needed to effect its capture? Was Alexander's intelligence or scouting service at fault, as it seems to have been before the Battle of Issus? He had not known where Darius and a huge Persian army was located before that battle, when he suddenly discovered its nearness. If Egypt was ready to fall like a ripe plum, why should Alexander not pass by Gaza and seize Egypt? Gaza might then have yielded without a fight. The old maxims about leaving enemy forts in one's rear or astride one's communications will not suffice to answer this question. Since Alexander had received the submission of all the Phoenician towns and conquered Tyre, his communications were safeguarded by sea as well as land. Was the attack on Gaza, a strong fort on an elevated position, motivated by stubbornness, or by a coherent logical plan?

Tyre had been captured for reasonable strategic ideas; even more difficult to attack than Gaza, this Phoenician island fortress was the possessor of the last remaining large fleet that might support the Persians and by sea attack harrass the Macedonian supply lines. Since the other Phoenician towns and fleets had submitted to Alexander, only the Tyrians could stir up trouble and perhaps even encourage the other Phoenicians to rebel. Alexander had to keep his sea lanes open to Greece and Macedonia, since his replacement troops and supplies came from there; and he still ruled Macedonia, while his deputy kept Greece subdued. With his sea lanes disrupted, Alexander could not send aid if all Greece revolted (as Sparta, in fact, did).

After his capture of the city of Miletus, Alexander then moved to dismiss his Greek fleet, or most of it, which seems odd. Arrian's reason for this mentions the need to save money, and the theory of defeating the Persian fleet "from the land" (which last sounds like reasoning after the fact).

Egypt may have remained defiant, and a less talented commander might well find himself in trouble if attacked in rear while he was attempting to attack Egypt. In the event, Gaza was captured, and Egypt surrendered without a fight, perhaps because the Persian administrators were discouraged by the Gaza result. It remains true that an enemy should be attacked at his weakest point, not at his strongest point, in the ordinary run of things. The "puzzle" of the Gaza attack may be a pseudo puzzle, and no real problem at all. Egypt must have seemed a more difficult conquest overall, and Gaza could be made into a supply depot for an Egyptian invasion after its occupation. This would remove an enemy force from the rear at the same time. And, if another large Persian army suddenly appeared in the north, a Macedonian garrison in Gaza might "lock up" Egypt and keep any Egyptian force out of subsequent events to the north.

Much more interesting is the question of shipping and food supply. The book *Alexander the Great and the Logistics of the Macedonian Army* by Engels reminds us of the paramount importance of food supply for an army, and the tremendous difficulties in obtaining such sufficient supply in the classical world.

We knew that the ancient harness for horses was inefficient and placed around the animals' necks in such a way as to cut off their breathing if they pulled against a heavy cart. D. W. Engels has reminded us that animals tend to eat up the supply of grain that they carry, so that food transportation was a problem. Troops could only live off the land by foraging to a limited extent, and not at all in barren places.

These factors have led scholars to stress the importance of ships in the classical world: only ships could carry very heavy loads of grain. This leads the present writer to suggest a new view of Alexander's famous strategy of "defeating the enemy fleet from the land".

If it is true, as does seem likely, that Alexander's army could transport only a few days' food supply with the troops, then this might give a new meaning to Alexander's march along the coast of Asia Minor, and his capture or "freeing" of the towns along the way. Did the ease of grain supply suggest his route?

Firstly, the country through which he made his march was

# Puzzles of Alexander the Great

never productive enough of grain to feed his army, so that periodic supply depots would have to be established along the way. This would entail the possession of towns or forts along the coast, so that supplies of grain could be brought in by water—for, again, only ships could carry very heavy loads of grain.

Secondly—due to the difficulty of transporting loads of grain in any large amounts from a stored depot once established—successive towns or forts would have to be secured as the army advanced. Towns held by Persian forces could be captured, and Greek towns under Persian rule could be "freed": which was part of the reason for the expedition in any event. Often Greek towns or cities contained an inner fort or citadel; these places would be made to order to store grain supplies shipped in for Alexander's army. As the army continued its progress, such depots would have to be set up in a series of forward steps. Greek towns that realized they would be freed by Alexander would surrender to him, thus obviating much trouble. In this view, Alexander's army followed the coastal route to the extent that it did in its initial campaigns in Asia Minor not just because the route was easier, or because of the theme of Greek vengeance against Persia, but also because this route provided coastal depots to be secured for the storage of supplies brought by sea. It would be advantageous to have depots supplied at each step forward, and this would result in greater difficulty for the enemy fleets if they attempted to stop such supplies. Only one port city might be an easy target for an enemy to watch and blockade. But if one possessed a number of port cities, the enemy fleets might leave gaps through which supplies could slip; it would be harder to blockade many places.

This seems to be contradicted by the fact of Alexander dismissing his fleet at a certain point, but we can perceive many possible motives. He may have already stocked large grain supplies; he may have wished to avoid a sea confrontation where the odds favored the Persian side (so as to avoid the possible loss of supply ships, and also avoid the deleterious propaganda results of a defeat); and most of all, he may have already been approached by emissaries from the Phoenician towns with secret offers of neutrality or even alliance as he approached their homes—if so, he would not wish his Greek fleet to fight with Phoenician units and endanger such hypothetical agreements.

The entire program would have the secondary effect of

# Beasts and Battles

"defeating the enemy fleets from the land" by preventing the enemy sailors from landing for food and water. Doubtless a good result, but it may have been caused by the Macedonian necessity to obtain food, and not by any particular plan or tactic of war. More than one good result of such a scheme fully justified its use: Alexander could get grain, free the Greek cities from the Persians, obtain strong points along the coast useful for the future, secure his sea communications to a greater extent, and reduce trouble from Darius' hired fleets by keeping them away from the coast. Multiple benefits accrued from the simple choice of a line of march: but was grain receipt the prime motive?

A peculiar puzzle about Alexander concerns the tactics of the Battle of Gaugamela (Arbela). This took place when Alexander, crossing a great, flat plain, encountered Darius' huge army that consisted of elephants, scythed chariots, cavalry, and masses of infantry. There are many puzzles arising from the accounts of the battle, which is neither completely nor clearly described. The surviving record contains mysteries and puzzles in itself. Modern historical descriptions are partially guesses.

Alexander ordered lanes in his army to open for scythe chariots to pass through without harming his men. That seems impossible. Scythed chariots were equipped with sharp blades attached to their hubs and/or wheel rims. Darius had two hundred of them. It seems very clever to have your army open lanes or aisles so that the chariots rush forward with the blades only cutting empty air, but can it be done? The chariot itself would have a certain width, and the blades protruding from its sides would make an even wider construct. One thinks of a width of at least fifteen to twenty feet. Lanes to be opened would have to be quite a bit wider.

The problem is lessened by the fact that there was provision for light-armed troops to stop most chariots in advance of the Macedonian front: the slingers, archers, and men who were especially assigned to the duty of stopping the horses seem to have put most of the chariots out of action. The remainder passed through the ranks without harm. That last is the problem.

Macedonian infantry phalanxes contained files of men that could consist of 120 men in line behind each other, with other files shoulder-to-shoulder on either side, reaching out to the distance, depending on the size of the army. The file of men could be reduced from 120 men to 8 (Robin Lane Fox, p. 76). These men carried a very long spear or lance, and the whole army must have resembled a rectangular pin-cushion from a distance. With a limited number of men against a larger foe, the reduction of the depth of the files of men behind each other from 120 to 8 would allow your army a wider front to more completely block a field, preventing the enemy from outflanking the ends of your line *if the field of battle was small enough in area.*

On the plain of the Battle of Gaugamela, Alexander would have been outflanked no matter how few men he put in the files, thinning them from front-to-back. Given the Persian advantage in numbers, he could not prevent the Persian front from extending past the ends of his lines, no matter what formation he adopted. That is the evident reason that he adopted a (possibly hollow) square or rectangular formation.

A very thin front less than 8 men deep might be easier to open, but probably could not be used because a thinned front could allow entry of the enemy cavalry into the formation, following the lanes made by the chariots, with disastrous effect. A very light front would also minimize the shock value of the phalanx at contact with the enemy line. But, the deeper the files, the more impossible it becomes to create aisles or lanes.

Darius may have fielded less than the 200 chariots on paper, but problems remain. The scholar Tarn deals with the problem by making the chariots go through the light-armed troops in advance of the main line that were stationed there against them, and gives no more thought to the matter (Tarn, W. W., *Alexander the Great*, Beacon Press, 1971 paperback, p. 49). However, the account generally considered best, that of the ancient Arrian (based largely on Ptolemy), has it that the chariots that got through the gaps were dealt with by grooms in the rear (Arrian, *The Campaigns of Alexander*, Penguin Books, 1984 paperback, p. 168); this reference may mean that the *cavalry* was the target of the chariots, or that there were grooms with remount horses behind the phalanx front and inside Alexander's hollow square. The chariots may have charged just the cavalry, or just the phalanx, or both.

In a simplified view, Alexander marched toward Darius with the front of his army composed of the thick lines of the phalanx, followed perhaps by an open space closed at the back by thinner

# Beasts and Battles

lines of infantry bringing up the rear (which had the ability to face to the rear if so ordered, creating in that direction a defense if needed). Cavalry made up the sides of this marching hollow square or hollow rectangle. The cavalry to the left was to fight a defensive battle, and the cavalry on the right was to make a decisive charge led by Alexander. Cavalry units were also placed so as to be sent outside and to the right flank of Alexander's troop, so as to hold off any Persian attack until Alexander could see an opening for his charge with his own unengaged troop that was kept free for that purpose.

These cavalry wings may have been reinforced with light-armed infantry insofar as they were to fight defensively, or even supported by regular infantry that further protected the sides of the formation. The supposed space behind the front of the leading phalanx may have contained light "baggage" in the form of spears and arrows, and remount horses controlled by "grooms". Or the "grooms" could have followed behind Alexander's right wing cavalry.

The square or rectangle formation was well constructed to repel charges by the numerous Persian cavalry, and all directions of approach were defended. If the guess at the "baggage" inside the moving formation was right, there was certainly another main "baggage" inside a camp some miles to the rear, from which the Macedonians had marched; also inside that camp were some prisoners, including Darius' mother. Various accounts that analyze the course of the battle sometimes propose an additional mystery: How could the Persian cavalry have raided this camp and baggage during the battle? There seems little mystery there. Alexander was not blockading a pass, but marching in a broad plain. In view of the Persian numbers of cavalry, he should not have detached any of his cavalry from the army to prevent any such raid even had he fore-knowledge of it—division of his forces would have been fatal. Indeed, in the course of the battle he is notified of an attack on his baggage, and his reply to the message is that his men should ignore the bags and fight the battle.

The close-packed body of the phalanx front in the center of the army always had enormous impact when it drove into an enemy line, but no matter how well-drilled, *it could not open lanes at once*, though it could do this if given time. Sometimes such gaps appeared when the phalanx advanced over uneven ground,

58

but they were unintentional and lessened the power of the phalanx's advance. When the chariots charged, the horses would run faster than men, and the charge would come quickly from a relatively short distance.

The only way that lanes or "aisles" could be formed in the phalanx is that *they were already formed as the army marched toward the enemy.* A thin line of light-armed men and archers or slingers in advance might mask the already formed lines from enemy view. But it may also be true that the phalanx was not charged by Persian chariots at all.

Alexander marched his army across the Persian front, moving toward the end of the Persian line on the Persian left. To prevent his further movement in that direction (and prevent danger to the Persian left flank), Persian cavalry intercepted the movement and attacked. Alexander met them with reserve units so as to hold them away from his own veteran cavalry which was waiting to charge at an opportune moment.

If the cavalry that Alexander led was the target of the chariots, it should be easier for this body to form open lanes quickly—certainly easier than for the phalanx. For one thing, the cavalry could expand to its right, since there was nothing outside its right flank—at least nothing until the Persian cavalry attacked and the reserve units met them and stopped their inroads. There are difficulties here, for the Persian cavalry attack might drive the Greek horse back into Alexander's waiting cavalry, thereby compressing his cavalry and making it impossible to open "lanes" against the chariots. The charge of the Persian horse would have to be met by the reserve units at a distance outside the regular right flank cavalry's area, and avoid being driven backward too far; or the chariots would have to have already been dealt with when the Persian cavalry charged. The charges of the enemy chariots and cavalry, if timed to work cooperatively, could represent a new and novel danger. Perhaps it came close and was just barely avoided, or perhaps the Persians had not seen the idea of using cavalry to force in and compress the opponent's right flank so as to make it a closely packed and confused mass as a target for the chariot charge. Such a compressed mass of men and horses could hardly be able to open lanes at all. The Persian cavalry do seem to have attacked just before, or at the same time as, the scythe chariots were launched (Tarn, p. 49, which follows Arrian's account in the timing of these Persian attacks).

The men stationed in front of the Macedonian front may have stopped most of the chariots, but the accounts that have come down to us indicate that some survived to reach their targets, but then passed through the famous lanes that opened to let them through. These may have been few, but are enough to set the logical problem here considered. Also of note is the way Alexander used his reserve cavalry units first in the battle, and saved the cavalry of his main strike force for use later. Thus his chief forces were "reserved"—held in hand until the right moment—and the reserve forces (perhaps better called "auxiliary forces"), were used first in the battle.

An interesting question arises when considering the charge forward of the phalanx. Firstly, since Darius was placed in the center of the Persian line (in most accounts), and Alexander charged back toward his position, there might be some danger of the infantry spearmen of the phalanx charging into the rear of their own cavalry. Secondly, the presence of the stalled or disabled chariots that the leading slingers or archers had stopped might break up the charge of the phalanx. It would have to find a way so that its real strength could be used, which was as a solid body impacting the enemy line, not as isolated units.

The scholars Fox (p. 234), and Wilcken both believed that some chariots charged the phalanx (Wilcken, Ulrich, *Alexander the Great*, translated by Richards, W. W. Norton, 1967 paperback; note to p. 68, line 9, is found on p. 331, mentioning the phalanx).

Disabled chariots in front of the Persian line would become obstacles. The phalanx would have to create different "lanes" to get around them and their blades, and then close ranks again so as to charge the opposing line as a solid front. More likely, the phalanx would continue marching until clear of stationary stalled chariots, so as to avoid confusion and fragmentation. (Those chariots create puzzles, even when out of action.)

If there was no empty area in the middle of Alexander's formation, and his army was marching as one solid mass structured as a moving square or rectangle, it seems even more impossible for the center infantry (the phalanx), to open lanes or gaps wide enough to pass enemy chariots. Again, only if such lanes were formed earlier, does it seem that they could suddenly "open" upon removal of a thin masking advance line.

With no vacant area between the front lines and rear lines, the "grooms" in the rear would probably be located behind Alexander's right flank cavalry—which might be indicated by the interesting statement that the Royal Guard aided the grooms in finishing off the few chariots that survived to pass through the lanes (Arrian, p. 168). This might also point to Alexander's cavalry on the right flank as the chariot target, but exact details will never be known. According to the captured Persian list of their order of battle, 100 scythe chariots were supposed to be stationed in front of their left, but actual strength may have been less; and few chariots would have passed the men in front detailed to deal with them. The men that actually were said to receive the charge of the chariots were stationed in front of the Companion cavalry on the right with Alexander; these were part of the Agrianians (probably light-armed troops), archers, and javelin-men commanded by Balacrus (Arrian, pp. 166, 168). This supports the view that *the cavalry alone* sustained the chariot attack. Rufus has the phalanx as the area of chariot attack, but his account seems less real in general than that of Arrian, at least concerning military matters.

Alexander may have *advanced obliquely* toward Darius' line with his left held back and right flank leading, because he was advancing and moving toward his right simultaneously—and such an approach would allow his left-flank cavalry to fight defensively while he and his right-flank cavalry made a decisive charge. If the accounts are right about this advance, then it points again to the chariots charging the right flank cavalry—simply because they were the units leading the advance. Such an advance would present yet more difficulties to the idea of "opening" lanes in the phalanx, especially if marching obliquely in semi-column.

Three clues point to the cavalry as chariot target: the mention of Royal Guard and grooms to the rear that dealt with a few chariots after their passage, difficulty in speedily opening a solid and numerous phalanx, and the fact that a slanted direction of advance must have meant that the cavalry would be in advance of the other troops and so nearest to the enemy. Arrian's description in Book Three (p. 168) seems clear, and supports this view, which therefore seems preferable—most scholars to the contrary notwithstanding.

# Beasts and Battles

There are more puzzles connected with accounts of the battle, but only one more will be considered here: Why did Alexander advance to his right (Darius' left wing)? No reason given is really adequate. Darius had smoothed some ground for use of his scythe chariots, and one reason given is that Alexander was for that reason making for rougher ground. That reason seems to fail because all scholars know that the phalanx itself worked best on smooth ground, and Alexander had already prepared his "open lane" defense. Another reason for the trend toward the right is given as avoidance of traps such as pits, stakes, or hidden trenches. But Darius would surely not have planted such traps in ground smoothed for the use of his own chariots—and he seems to have ordered the chariots forward before the Macedonians had marched out of the smooth prepared area. The ancient authors' views that Alexander was avoiding something seem wrong, if avoidance of a physical thing was meant, as it appears they intended. A more reasonable view might be that he was avoiding giving his enemy an idea of where in their line he might attack.

Alexander's army had rested all night at a distance, while Darius' army had remained in arms and awake all night, fearing a night attack. Darius' troops were in a defensive and fixed position as Alexander approached. Therefore *Alexander and his Macedonians and Greeks could arrive at the battlefield at any point they wished, and probably did.* Alexander would not have come to the field and then taken defensive measures; he was probably not avoiding types of ground or possible traps *after* he arrived. He could have arrived at the field on the rougher ground had he wished to do so. The old arguments are not valid.

Robin Lane Fox's *Alexander the Great* (p. 237) lists more than one motive, though one might have some doubts about the motive of avoidance of being outflanked, remembering the formation already created against this contingency. And also remembering that (given the sizes of the two armies), the Persians could always encircle or outflank the Greeks—the reason for the square or rectangular defense array in the first place. But it is true that a move to the right would make the flanking forces extend further out, and prevent most of the Persian infantry from coming into contact (with the result that most of the Persian foot soldiers would remain useless and not take part until the battle was lost). This last thought may have been too simple for the ancient authorities, with their "traps" and "rough ground"; but one should always rememmber that such opinions represent *defensive* thinking, whereas Alexander was on the attack—and with the initiative. He was trying to flank the Persians, not just avoid that himself, for he was active while they were passive, with the exception of their masses of cavalry.

The obvious reason for the slant to the right was that the aim was to reach the extreme left of the Persian line and then roll up its line by a combination of phalanx and cavalry attack. If, as we are told, Darius' best-drilled troops were probably in the center of his line, the general mass of his infantry was likely to be static and not very maneuverable.

A faint possibility for a slant to the right might be to disguise the point of attack, which may have been the person of Darius himself. Though that is possible, it seems to be less likely than the simple aim of beginning the destruction of the Persian army first. Because Alexander perceived a chance to charge Darius does not prove such a charge or even point of attack to be the original intention: it may have been simple opportunism.

There is a slim chance that Darius was positioned in or behind the Persian left wing. He was "supposed" to be in the center of the line according to majority scholarly opinion, that opinion being based ultimately on the accounts of the captured list of the Persian order of battle. But there is a minority opinion preserved in the writings of Quintus Curtius Rufus (*The History of Alexander*, Penguin Books, 1984 paperback; see pp. 83, 85,—his Book Four). Rufus puts Darius on the left wing, and in command of it. Now we see the opinion of attack on Darius himself as the reason for the move to the right. The placement of as many as 100 chariots on the Persian left may indicate that they had studied Alexander's tactics, and perceived that he usually attacked from his own right flank, but it is possible that the account in Rufus puts Darius on that flank because it was known that Alexander charged him. This minority opinion of the position of Darius may be just another example of "reasoning after the fact", but it does make events clearer and more easily understood for a variety of reasons. Rufus' account of events involving the Battle of Gaugamela seems jumbled and disjointed, though colorful and vivid. It is not very useful for descriptions of battle tactics. But in the one aspect of the position of Darius, Rufus might be correct.

# Beasts and Battles

Alexander might have marched in the direction of some "trap" area so that he would seem to be doing what the Persians desired. In that way he could avoid being unduly harried by the Persian cavalry, and could veer away toward his true goal of the Persian left—"rough ground" being irrelevant—at the last minute, when he was sure that he was close enough to the enemy to bring his powerful infantry phalanx into action against them.

In any event, if he could reach the extreme left end of the Persian line with his more maneuverable army, he could bring more men to bear against fewer—he could outnumber the enemy at the point of attack, even though their entire force outnumbered him. This flank attack with his veterans against men "drafted" could roll down the Persian line with crushing effect; the Persian infantry on the flanks being less likely to be well-drilled, and likely to be confused and panicked by such an attack, probably would be unable to meet it properly.

If Darius was on the left wing in front of Alexander's right wing, then when Alexander charged, it would be more straight ahead—and not back toward the Persian center (and in front of his own phalanx?). And, again, if the chariots had charged *just the cavalry* on the Macedonian right flank, then not only could the horses open "lanes" more quickly than infantry packed tight, but another thing of importance would occur: the phalanx could charge straight ahead without having to go around disabled chariots. *Was Alexander, himself, the chief chariot target?*

There are many doubts. Wilcken (*Alexander the Great*, pp. 134-135), believed that Alexander did not make a square or rectangular formation, but rather a *potential* square or rectangle. He thought that the phalanx made the front, with cavalry on each side, and another line of infantry at the rear—and that there were additional infantry on each side of the phalanx between the cavalry and the central phalanx. These "added" men would extend his line of battle, but could drop back on each side and fill in the side of a square or rectangle at need. In another difference, we note that Rufus in his *History* made Alexander's basic formation a circle (p. 82), and not a square or rectangle.

In connection with the idea of the chariots charging the cavalry instead of the phalanx, we might note Alexander's caution to his "wing" commanders (Rufus, p. 82), to extend the line sideways, but not at the expense of the rear ranks. And especially note his caution for their "not to become compressed" on the wings (p. 82). A warning not to weaken the rear seems to point unmistakably to infantry, for cavalry would not be in rear or behind the phalanx—it was always kept on the flanks (each side of the line allowing the horses more freedom of unhindered movement). Perhaps these words of Rufus point to Wilcken's thinned line of foot soldiers on each side of the phalanx and inside the cavalry; these may be the troops that Wilcken thought *could have* completed the side defenses of a formation if needed. But, bearing in mind Rufus' statement that the "phalanx" was charged by the chariots (p. 86), these may represent some few infantry, though not phalanx proper, that were included in the chariot attack. A thin line that did not "become compressed" might have the ability to open the requisite lanes. Fill-in troops, used to make the front longer, might be involved instead of the phalanx, and so make the old accounts more believable. And, as an added bonus, the phalanx would not have to detour around any stalled bladed chariots that might otherwise blunt its charge by breaking up its formation and thus reducing its power. It seems questionable anyhow to hold that chariots would ever be sent to charge a solid walking mass of men with heads of long lances protruding from their front. Even the more mobile cavalry units could not hope to make such a frontal attack succeed. (It would not be attempted until tried by medieval armored knights—only to fail even then if the infantry spearmen took proper action. Cavalry charges might succeed against Roman infantry from time to time, because the Romans fought with their basic weapon—the short sword—after they had thrown their javelins; to charge a wall of spears or even longer lances would be another matter entirely.)

There is an odd but unlikely motive for an advance trending toward the Persian left that is never considered by writers who comment on the battle. And most such writers know of the facts of this possibility, but have refused to mention it in this particular connection. The Persian captured list of their order of battle indicated the presence of elephants. Many writers have remarked that the scent of elephants terrifies horses unused to the smell, and might make cavalry useless. Was Alexander aware of this fact, and was he attempting to move upwind of elephants? A peculiar motive that no one has considered, and perhaps not probable. It may be that the elephants "on paper" did not make it to the scene of the battle. At any rate, they were not on the Persian left. And now it is far too late to sniff out an answer, at least insofar as the puzzle of elephant presence is concerned.

There is danger in picking out from ancient sources just what statements seem useful for the clarification of ancient events, and that danger is clearly realized. This caution must be matched by the realization that the ancient sources quite often overlook very simple things, and sometimes give opinions or reasons for things that verge upon the silly or ludicrous. And they quite often "explain" the motives for actions by reasoning backwards from results.

It is doubtful that a chariot, however armed, would charge a phalanx. It is doubtful that a phalanx could "open lanes" in an immediate reaction to an order. It is doubtful that Alexander the Great would arrive on a battlefield at "the wrong part" of it and have to march sideways to correct his "error".

The result of the movements is well known: the Persians sent cavalry to prevent Alexander's further progress toward their left flank, Alexander sent reserve cavalry to beat these away from his own main strike force horse; Persian movements of their cavalry opened a gap in their lines near Darius' position, and Alexander took that moment to charge into the gap, eventually winning the battle after some hard cavalry fighting. Darius fled when he saw Alexander forcing his way ever nearer. (Or, if those reports were made to flatter Alexander, Darius may have fled when he perceived that the battle was indeed going to be lost—as Mark Antony did at the later naval battle of Actium.) The fact of Darius' flight hastened the end of the battle when other Persian forces followed his example, and Alexander and his soldiers had won a brilliant victory.

An obscure victory in its details in many ways, though clear-cut in its effects, leading Greek exploration all the way through India with its rhinocerous-unicorn and its cockatrice-king cobra, animals that remained long in the imagination of the West. Ideals of empire were set within men's heads; and the Romans, emulating Alexander, achieved what his successors failed to do, and became noticeable in history.

Despite recent attention to the requirements for food supply of ancient armies, it may be that the requisite deductions have not

## Puzzles of Alexander the Great

been drawn from these studies. Thus, Alexander's "delays" might be to some extent caused by two reasons: (1) the need to wait for a grain harvest, and (2) the need to pause while the supplies of grain were transported to depots so as to be safe and yet available at need for his army. The question of food supply at Persepolis noted by D. W. Engels (see above, p. 52), might well be applied also to the wait at Tyre, and perhaps to some extent to the time of his illness before the Battle of Issus.

The power of the Persian Empire at its height was unable to deal with guerillas, and the Persians paid wild hill shepherds to prevent their attacks. Alexander solved the problem of guerilla war by refusing to pay. He captured the guerilla's homes and villages by surprise in winter—and made peace with them, and made a treaty whereby they paid him taxes in the form of livestock. Alexander solved his problems quickly and with ease, because of his talent. Much later, in a different age, we follow his history haltingly, and wonder at his success.

# ▶ 6 ◀

# NOAH'S ARK LOCATED?

Deep inside Turkey, close to its eastern borders with Iran and the Soviet Union, there is a place which excites curiosity. It is said that there is an ancient ship on a mountain, almost covered by a glacier. This ship is thought by some to be "Noah's Ark". The Russian Tsar was said to have sent an expedition to that place: reportedly, they had found a wooden structure containing iron bars. The Tsar fell from power shortly thereafter, and any reports from the mission were hidden, lost, or destroyed. Could this really exist, could it be a ship, and could it be Noah's ship?

There are many hoaxes in subjects of a sensational nature. We remember the "petrified" man called the Cardiff Giant, which many years ago was exhibited in the United States, and which was discovered to have been a statue carved in a distant state, transported to a farmer's field, and secretly buried so that it could be "discovered" later and seem to be genuine. We remember the famous scientific hoax of the "Piltdown Man", a fabricated skull created by joining together ape and human parts (hoaxer unknown). And, apparently, the "Bigfoot" subject includes much hoaxed evidence (see Kenneth Wylie's *Bigfoot*, Viking Press, New York, 1980, p. 140). Finally, we have recently seen evidence that the famous "Shroud of Turin" is a fabrication from approximately 600 years ago instead of 2000 years in the past. Whatever the motive (including ego gratification, financial gain, practical jokes, or a desire to publicize a cause), it is clear that one must guard against fakery.

# Noah's Ark Located?

In the case of the claimed "Noah's Ark" phenomenon, there are many reports going back through centuries, and not just one or a few. The interesting book by Charles Berlitz, *The Lost Ship of Noah: In Search of the Ark at Ararat*, (Ballantine Books, Fawcett edition, New York, 1988 paperback), notes reports from many sources and various times; his first six chapters are informative, with the latter part of the book more devoted to a somewhat speculative religious content.

Throughout history many peoples have passed through or had influence upon the area in which this mountain—"Mount Ararat" on modern American maps—is found. Scythians, Persians, Armenians, Romans (who campaigned far into Asia Minor according to Plutarch, though perhaps past the borders of their empire), the Pontic Kingdom, Parthians, Byzantines, Ottoman Turks, and others all passed near the area in question in their time. Berlitz, himself, mentions an ancient boat that some early ruler kept on a lake in the area (Berlitz, pp. 50-51), though it is indicated that this boat, however large, is not the "Ark"—which is located elsewhere and higher up (Berlitz, pp. 57, 78).

On the south coast of the Black Sea there is an ancient city of Greek origin (from probably the 8th century B.C.), located about one hundred miles from the eastern end of that Sea. This is modern Trabzon (ancient Trapezus), which in olden days was the northern end of a trade route leading toward the south, to Armenia and Mesopotamia (cf. Michael Grant's *The Rise of the Greeks*, Charles Scribner's Sons, New York, 1988, pp. 270-271). It is well known that the north coast of the Black Sea (ancient Euxine) in ancient times exported considerable amounts of grain in commerce, but Grant points out another major item of export (among others), from the north across the Black Sea: slaves, sad to say (M. Grant, pp. 272, 275, 307).

Mount "Ararat" is more east-south-east from Trabzon than south. Yet it is conceivable that other trade routes led past the place now called "Mount Ararat", running toward the Black Sea, and some leading in more southerly directions toward Iran (ancient Persia), and Mesopotamia. Berlitz's book exhibits a map following the Title Page in which a site near "Great Ararat" is marked as "Ruins of CaravanSaray" (which we take to be a not-too-ancient trade route stop for caravans).

If there is an anomalous structure on the mountain or near

# Beasts and Battle

it, it might be a ruin of an ancient "slave pen"; one might expect such a structure to be near a glacier (providing water), and to have iron bars for obvious reasons—and probably to be located not too high up on a mountain unless on or near a pass. But even more likely is a multi-purpose structure which could be used also as *animal pens* for trans-shipment to the cities and towns of the Roman Empire.

The many towns and cities of the Roman Empire used animals in the "games" of their amphitheatres. Many places had these amphitheatres in addition to the large and well-known Flavian Amphitheatre (Colosseum) at Rome. Animals were not only matched in battle, but were also used in large numbers in so-called "hunts", in which many were killed in arenas. An example of such an "animal hunt" is found in Suetonius' account of the life of Julius Caesar, (Suetonius, *The Twelve Caesars*, Penguin Books, New York, 1987 paperback, p. 31).

Considering the large numbers of animals that would be required for such "hunts", the existence of a holding pen for animals on a trade route leading to the Black Sea would almost be expected. Many goods in the ancient world that reached the cities around the Mediterranean Sea or the Black Sea would come by water.

The slave trade lasted from ancient times, through the Viking era, and down through later centuries. So it seems that the idea of a "holding pen" or stop-over place for captives from north of the Black Sea cannot be discounted. Even after the fall of the Western Roman Empire, such a structure could continue to see use, perhaps then chiefly for shipping slaves south for money. The word "slave", as many scholars believe, is derived from the word for "Slav" (as in "Slavic People"; see e.g. Henri Pirenne, *A History of Europe*, Vol. I, Doubleday Anchor Books, New York, 1956 paperback, p. 64); a derivation evocative of tragic past events in history.

The entire question of such a structure presupposes that one does exist. Accepting that a structure *of some type* does exist, could it have survived from antiquity? The answer may be "yes". We know that Roman ships or barges survived from long ago, sunk on the bottom of a fresh-water lake; they were found prior to World War II when the lake was drained. A structure encased in ice could also last a long time. The books and television programs concerned

## Noah's Ark Located?

with the "Ark" question uniformly suppose that the structure is mostly or even entirely encased in ice, which thaws somewhat in summer. While most wooden structures would crumble into dust through the centuries, a structure so sealed might well be preserved; this long-term preservation is by no means impossible.

The structure indicated in Berlitz's book is located *very high* on the mountain, with some wood beams being seen almost at the summit (Berlitz, pp. 57, 78, 87). If this is so, the idea of a slave pen or animal pen seems to be unlikely.

The area might have been subject to geologic uplift over time, and the climate may have changed also. But even if the area is subject to earthquake (as is much of Turkey), it is unlikely that a ship used by some ancient king on a lower level was subsequently carried to a tremendous height of, for instance, 15,000 feet, by geological forces. If the "Ark" (or whatever the structure), is located around that height (Berlitz, pp. 57, 78), then we are not very much inclined to believe that the object in or under the glacier is a ship at all. And some reports of beams of wood *near the summit* (Berlitz, p. 87), make that view even more doubtful.

Could some Persian Great King of the empire later overthrown by Alexander the Great have owned a "summer palace" at this place? The mountain is apparently an uncomfortable, and even dangerous place. Aside from rock-slides, snow-covered crevasses, wild animals such as wolves and bears, and poisonous serpents at its base, Greater Ararat is apparently the scene of frequent electrical storms (Berlitz, pp. 55, 59, 78), creating much danger for climbers. All this makes a summer palace, or even a high fort, unlikely; and the high air has too little oxygen.

There is a possibility, so far unmentioned, that might account for a wooden structure high on the mountain. Even in the dim days of prehistory, high places were thought to be "holy" and full of magic. The ancient Canaanites and Israelites seem to have had such views. And the Sumerians with their ziggurats with shrines at the top may have held such beliefs (as noted by C. Leonard Woolley in *The Sumerians*, W. W. Norton, N. Y., 1965 paperback, p. 141).

Berlitz (p. 13), has an account of a monastery that was buried by earthquake or lava flow in 1840, along with a native town. Later, on p. 78, he mentions a monastery still operating nearby. Could the "Ark" be a monastery? And why constructed of wood instead of the rocks and stones that abound in the area, and all over the mountain? Again, the answer may have been given in Berlitz's book: the people with knowledge of the area seem to believe that rocks of granite type attract the lightning (p. 55); if the ancients believed this, they might well decide to build with wood.

In 1955, a Frenchman named Navarra reportedly extracted wood samples from the claimed "Ark" structure high on the mountain of Greater Ararat, and after carrying them out of Turkey had them analyzed scientifically by radio-carbon dating and other methods (Berlitz, pp. 80-84). Two of the reported dates give the age of the wood as very much in the Christian era of the ancient world: 1250 years old, and A.D. 560 (p. 83); from the year 1955 the date of 1250 years old would indicate an origin in about 705 A.D. These two dates of the 6th and 8th centuries are given as from American testing laboratories, but dates much earlier from Egyptian and European institutions are cited: dates such as 4000, 5000, and 6000 years old (Berlitz, p. 83). We are not told if these dates have been calibrated with tree-ring findings, which would act to extend backward in time the radio-carbon dates (although only a few years would be added to a date of 2000 years old), and we are also not given the standard "plus or minus" figures usually accompanying radio-carbon dating.

Taking the above dates at face value with the cautions just noted, we can make a few comments. The earlier dates, especially that of 6000 years ago, more or less fit modern views of the approximate time of the beginnings of Sumerian civilization, and the date of 5000 years ago roughly corresponds to what modern scholars view as the beginnings of writing in Sumerian locations near the Persian Gulf. If the "American" dates are correct, and we are talking of the early eighth century A.D. or the mid sixth century A.D., then we are talking of the time after the fall of the Western Roman Empire, and the early medieval period; for a time so recent, very few "bristlecone pine years" based on tree rings need be added (if they have not already been figured into the "American" dates), in order to lengthen the radio-carbon findings to the proper age—the dates from the University of California and the University of Pennsylvania would leave no chance for the wood samples to be any older than the Christian era. (We are here taking the printed reports in Berlitz pp. 80-84 at face value, and presuming them to be well based and valid, for purposes of discussion.) *If these*

# Noah's Ark Located?

*"American" dates are correct, then the structure from which they came cannot be "Noah's Ark".* If the more ancient dates are correct (those from Egypt, France, and Spain), then the trees were cut in the times of the Assyrians, Babylonians, or even the Sumerians.

Can we be talking of some sort of monastic structure? By becoming a monk one avoided paying taxes, avoided having to serve in armies, avoided having to sell oneself into slavery to pay one's debts, avoided being "chained to the land" to work someone else's farm as a serf—and could express any genuine religious feelings at the same time. The map in Berlitz's book following the Title Page shows a forest in the Ararat area, a possible source of timber that may have been larger in the past. Monasteries were often situated in places difficult of access, and sometimes even fortified. The monks were not only nearer to heaven on high places, but chiefly they were able to avoid passing armies with all the attendant problems of such encounters. The area of Mount Ararat is located in what used to be an area of influence of the Byzantine Empire; while Rome in the West might be said to have fallen in 476 A.D., Rome in the East did not fall until 1453 A.D. A place far up on a mountain would be safer from steppe nomads, for horses would not be at their best on steep slopes with rock-slides and snow-covered crevasses. The horse nomads were dangerous and best avoided, remembering the tales of piles of human heads stacked up by their armies (can it be true that one of the Mongol khans briefly entertained the idea of killing all the Chinese to make a broader pasture for his horses, until being reminded of the possibilities of taxation?). Even the ancient Scythian nomads made goblets of the skulls of adversaries they had killed in battle.

Could some religious abbot have caused a monastery to be built in the shape of an "ark", under the conviction that the world would end at some certain time, and thus he and his fellow monks might be saved by such a symbol, or in event of "another Flood"? We dislike to believe that a false "Ark" might be constructed simply in order to enrich the locals financially through pilgrim visits.

There have been many floods throughout the past, and the land of Mesopotamia doubtless had more than its fair share. It was from that land, home of the Sumerians and later Babylonians, that a tale of an early "Noah" figure spread. The Greeks also had their "world-wide" flood, with their survivor of a different name.

But the Mesopotamian stories of the Deluge would take

place prior to the advent of the Iron Age, and various accounts of the structure in the glacier mention iron in connection with it. The Iron Age in Europe did not begin until the 7th century: in the 600's B.C. The Hittite people and those near their land had iron many centuries earlier, but even this early use of iron would (taking the Biblical accounts seriously), be far too late to be linked with a theoretical "Noah". *Any structure containing iron could not be Noah's Ark*, according to our best modern knowledge of the past, and accepting the ancient Mesopotamian tale of a universal deluge at face value for the moment.

If at some early time, a Sumerian native built a large boat early and escaped a local flood, such a boat would probably be constructed of reeds (as were early houses in the area); and would long since have crumbled to dust, as pointed out by L. Sprague de Camp (private communication).

If we consider that the ziggurats of Mesopotamia might have been somehow connected with the beliefs of early peoples about the "sacred" nature of high places, mountain shrines seem possible. Such beliefs in early Palestine have long been well attested, and we know that mountain climbers from the West that entered Tibet and Nepal to climb and explore encountered native views that the high mountains such as Everest were the home of the gods. Such beliefs are not rare or novel, but widespread.

There may have been a pre-Christian shrine to some god or goddess that lies on the mountain-side under the ice, unexplored by archaeologists. The very presence of the electrical storms cited by Berlitz may have made the mountain seem more sacred to prehistoric peoples, and perhaps to later Christians. Pagan temples or shrines were sometimes built in or near places having odd physical attributes. One such was located near an ancient cave in Turkey thought to be an entrance to Hades in the period of the Greeks and Romans; the cave apparently exuded carbon dioxide, and animals within or too near it died quickly. Next to the cave was a temple in the Greco-Roman city of ancient Hierapolis (in Pammukkale, region or Denizli, Turkey: see a description in the journal *Antiquity* of March, 1988, Vol. 62, No. 234, pp. 88-89; report by Cross and Aaronson). The priests of the temple could enter the cave with impunity by holding their breath. Some believed that the Delphic Oracle used a vapor issuing from the earth, or perhaps some sort of incense burned in a place below by priestly attend-

## Noah's Ark Located?

ants. In any event, a mountain that "threw lightning bolts" in addition to being a mysterious high place already, might be a likely site for an ancient shrine, if not for a Christian monastery. We recall that the chief Greek god Zeus was thought to cast thunderbolts. And the Greek gods lived high up on Mount Olympus. Berlitz notes accounts of "Arks" on several mountains (e.g. pp. 151-152). He also mentions an ancient ship in Armenia in the third century B.C., and reported again toward the end of the first century A.D., citing notations by Berossus and Josephus, respectively (Berlitz, p. 8). These citations mention scrapings of bitumen used as or in amulets by the natives. There may, then, possibly be some structure to the north of Babylon—perhaps located in Syria, Armenia, or Turkey—dating from early times; some sort of pagan shrine.

*The idea of a shrine* seems more convincing for an anomalous structure of wood high on the side or top of a mountain. A place sacred to preceding pagan cultures could easily enough remain sacred under Christian auspices later; a Christian shrine could be built upon a pagan sacred spot, as sometimes Christian churches were built upon pagan temple sites. The ancient regard for high places already noted above makes this conceivable.

A monastery would probably be built lower down, within walking distance of the shrine, and this may have been the case of the monastery mentioned by Berlitz that was swallowed by an earthquake on Ararat (Berlitz, p. 13). Ancient reported "Arks" from many locations may represent legendary memories of shrines in high places throughout Mesopotamia and adjacent areas—but admittedly that is a speculative guess.

It is not at all clear why any edifice upon a mountain—whatever its purpose—should take the form of a ship. There were few reasons to build anything upon a great height. Aside from a shrine (our guess here), a fort, a monastery, or a watch-tower equipped with fire-beacon, there was virtually no reason to be high on a mountain. Mountain-climbing as a sport was unknown to prior ages. The ancient Hittites worshipped a Weather God; but even more to the point is a report in Herodotus (*Persian Wars*, I, 131; Modern Library edition, p. 73), of Persians performing religious rites on the summits of high mountains. Could a precinct have been constructed for some such *temporary occupation by worshippers?*

## Beasts and Battle

The reports concerning some structure or structures on or near the mountain seem to provide a reason for a careful scientific investigation of the places involved. There are *claims of two different boat-shapes in the area*, one high on the mountain, and another at a lower level and some distance away (Berlitz, pp. 50-51, 150).

The mention of "iron", plus the age data produced by the "American" analysis of the wood samples, seem to exclude the more elevated structure from any chance of being "Noah's Ark", even on that story's own terms. More data is needed.

Is there a structure on the mountain? If so, can it have caused the mountain to be given the name "Ararat"? Can the ruins of an ancient shrine have become identified with the beliefs of a later age? We cannot be sure without a better investigation.

# ▶ 7 ◀

# ACHILLES AND THE TORTOISE: A RIDDLE SOLVED?

Achilles was a very fast runner. Among the Greek warriors attempting to seize the town of Troy, the people called "Achaians" in Homer's *Iliad*, there was unlikely to be anyone faster in a footrace.

The tortoise is a very slow creature, not very speedy in movement. In a race held between the two, Achilles would be sure to win—one might say that there would be no contest in such a match.

But a very ancient thinker named Zeno produced a puzzle that said (in effect): If you give the tortoise a head start, then Achilles can never catch him! All that is required is that the tortoise leave first.

This is the reason: in the time it takes Achilles to move a short distance, the tortoise will have moved a short distance more. Achilles can never make up the initial distance between them, for each time he moves to cover part of that distance, the tortoise will use the same time to increase the distance, even though the increase that he achieves is a very short length (for the tortoise is a very slow mover). Each time Achilles moves, the tortoise moves—only more slowly than the man.

If a person considers this situation mentally, making a sort of "mental picture" of the process at work here, it will be seen at once that the distance between the two will become less and less, as they both move "at the same time"; and, equally, the time of each spurt of movement will become less and less. Achilles will move closer and closer to the tortoise, *but he will never catch him.*

Achilles will never win such a "race". Not only can he never pass the tortoise, he cannot even catch up with him—again supposing that the tortoise is given a head start. He will get closer and closer, in a shorter and shorter time. But he will fail in this "race". Why?

What could account for this peculiar logical result?

Let us perform a brief analysis of the structure of this problem: we will call it a "structural analysis". If the problem seems insoluble, perhaps it is within the structure of the problem itself that we may find some sort of logical answer. The problem itself seems to be insoluble by logic, and on the face of it might be destined to forever remain a paradox whose nature cannot be discerned.

Back to our structural analysis: What are the basic terms of this problem? This should give us a clue to its nature. *The basic terms of this problem are Space and Time.* We will name these terms basic components. Consider these components of Time and Space further. How are they described? *They are described in terms of the Space and Time between Achilles and the tortoise.* The key word is "between".

The whole of Space or Time (especially the former), is not involved in the overall problem, but only the space between the "racers". The time involved is linked to and conditioned by the space covered in what might be called each "step of movement" or "period of progress".

Note the description: *"In the time it takes ... "* Achilles to move x distance, the Tortoise will have moved y distance. Running this process through the "mental image", it is clear that the *distance* between the two will become shorter and shorter, and the *time* involved in each of these periods or steps of movement will become shorter and shorter. The time periods progressively become shorter, so that the time passes more and more quickly.

What is happening here? As the basic components of the problem, Space and Time, become more and more reduced (trend-

# Achilles and the Tortoise: A Riddle Solved?

ing toward less and less of each), *the problem is tending to disappear!* Because of the trick of setting the problem's components in terms of the Time and Distance *between the racers* instead of a more "normal" Time and Space encompassing them and passing behind them as well as beside them and in front of them. As the time passes more and more quickly with each segment of action, so the Space or Distance between the protagonists becomes progressively less and less.

But it now becomes clear to us why Achilles can never catch the tortoise. He is not allowed to do so by the way that the problem is constructed. Just short of reaching his adversary, Achilles will run into what we might call an "infinity" situation: the problem will become blocked by an infinity blockade: the Space or Distance *will move progressively toward the infinitely small,* and so will the Time involved in each of Achilles' strides as he comes close to the tortoise.

At this point, infinity stands just between Achilles and the tortoise, and it is now clear that the "problem" can never be solved (to the extent that Achilles cannot ever be made to catch the tortoise). Looked at another way, the basic components of the problem are set forth in such a way that, by becoming less and less in magnitude as one considers the problem in process, the basic components of the problem tend to disappear. The problem might be considered to be in process of vanishing while one is in process of "solving" it. Or, as indicated above, it might be said that we have run into what might be seen as an *infinity blockade.*

We have not solved the paradox. We seem to have demonstrated that it *cannot be solved,* which is progress, in a way. Zeno has produced a trick situation to puzzle us. A very clever production, but still a trick. Computers cannot ever "solve" this riddle, for obvious reasons.

There may be a whole class of conundrums in which the "infinity block" occurs. How many students in high school have been confronted with the following puzzle:

Consider a triangle with its base resting on the ground, and its two equal sides making an apex in the air above (or, for a large triangle, with its apex in outer space, perhaps). Each base angle is to be almost a right angle—just barely short of 90°. (There "must be" a maximum angle that would yet still be just short of making a full right angle.)

# Beasts and Battles

But, for any angle you care to create, it can be made larger by simply moving the point where the two sides meet a further distance upward (or out into space, depending on how large the beginning triangle is). The "infinity block" here occurs in the fact that you can move the point of the triangle upwards an infinite number of times.

Such an infinity trap or block could conceivably have a person going around in circles mentally for a long time, like a dog chasing his tail. Doubtless such a trap occurs in various other situations—perhaps a whole class of puzzles contain a hidden or disguised "infinity trap".

Many things that the ancient Greeks did seem puzzling when first encountered, and some of those things, ideas, and presentations are tricks. Sometimes a structural analysis will allow us to penetrate into what makes a puzzle "tick", as in the case just noted of the seeming paradox of Achilles and the Tortoise.

Another such puzzle is somewhat simpler in structure, but also contains a trick to make us stop and think for a moment. Out of their love of the play with words and clever witticisms, the Greeks manufactured the following bit of logic, which we will imitate in a make-believe conversation here:

Mr. A: You have a dog, don't you?

Mr. B: Yes, a fine male dog good for hunting.

Mr. A: Has he produced any puppies?

Mr. B: Yes, with the aid of a female.

Mr. A: You would agree that this performance means that he is now a father of those pups?

Mr. B: Yes, but so what?

Mr. A: You own him, of course?

Mr. B: Yes.

Mr. A: Then he is both yours and a father?

Mr. B: Obviously, yes.

Mr. A: We have shown the dog to be your father, have we not?

Mr. B: Wait a minute—you're not calling me an S.O.B., are you?

Mr. A: No, just joking; but can you show that the logic here is wrong?

What has been happening here? Well, for one thing, the words "your father" have been employed in a way not usually encoun-

# Achilles and the Tortoise: A Riddle Solved?

tered. But the main thing seems to be that these words perform a neat trick: here we have an instance of use of the same words to point to two different things. In terms of the context, we have a description of something (the dog), that one owns—combined with an indication of one's relationship with another person. Something that an animal has done has been confused with a person's family relationship. The brevity of the two words creates a sort of mental confusion by causing a thought that points in two different directions at the same time. The two different directions of meaning could have been untangled by the use of further words that "pinned down" the meaning, but the intention is not to clarify the thought; in fact the idea is to create a pseudo-puzzle—a trick situation meant to make us laugh, and perhaps to briefly confuse us. (The fake logic conversation above is loosely based on Plato's "Euthydemus" dialogue from Vol. 1, *The Dialogues of Plato*, Random House, New York, 1937, p. 161).

The confusion created in our mind by the deliberate confusion of two different things or approaches in combination can make us pause and set us puzzles. Such combinations will not normally occur, but may be forced together by a witty person: and then they set a puzzle for us. Some artists have used such a forced combining of different intellectual contexts to create witty visual puzzles. For instance, there are two different ways to indicate height in a picture. The first way is one that might be called the naive way. Children make pictures in such a way that "up" is shown simply by placing things toward the top of a piece of paper; anything so placed is "higher" than a thing drawn nearer the bottom of the paper. The sky is perhaps indicated by a scrawl of blue near or at the top of the paper, and the ground by some brown or green color near or at the bottom of the paper. From this simple way of looking at things, we have (from the overall look of the picture), a way to "see" things as "higher" or "lower" than other things portrayed. We might call this simple and natural way of looking at a painting or drawing a "natural" convention; we are expected to see the picture a certain way as regards relative heights of objects depicted.

Another way of showing objects in relation to each other within the picture was developed during the Renaissance in Italy: the convention of perspective viewing of a picture. This way of seeing, or convention of how we are expected to "see" a picture is quite different from the "natural" convention, insofar as some-times things shown near the top of a picture could be considered as depicted "lower" or "nearer the ground" than other items placed nearer the bottom of the picture. Such a case would depend upon the placement of one's viewpoint: if eye level is placed high up (from a cliff top, for example, looking down and outward toward the horizon), then an item (perhaps a tree) placed near the foot of the cliff and nearer to the theoretical viewer, might well be "taller" and reach "higher" than a boulder placed nearer the ho-rizon and further away from the viewer. The boulder would be physically higher up on the flat piece of paper or canvas, but the visual convention of perspective viewing will result in its being seen as less "tall" than the tree. It will not be seen as reaching higher into the air than the tree, if we adopt a "perspective" view. The use of perspective by the artist allows us to clearly discern the relative heights of objects depicted.

Both these ways of seeing a picture are really conventions, and each has its "rules" or ways we are expected to approach the picture. The natural" way of presenting objects as higher or lower is simply to place the objects nearer the bottom or nearer the top of the picture. In the "perspective" way, it all depends on the theoretical placement of the observer's viewpoint in relation to the horizon line.

Some artists have produced witty pictures by the combi-nation of these two conventions (or ways of seeing). If perspective convention is conjoined with a natural "up-down" convention, the artist can produce some puzzling visual effects that make us scratch our heads in confusion. The artist Escher seems to have sometimes produced the witty and puzzling effects of objects por-trayed doing "impossible" things relative to each other; and the method by which this could be done is the deliberate use of *both* conventions we have described in the same picture. Normally these ways of looking at pictures are mutually exclusive. Since they do involve different principles of "how we see", it is not logical to use them together (except as a joke, or witticism). Their deliberate joining can puzzle us for a few moments, until we think about the *structure* of the conventions that the artist is using. Either con-vention makes sense when used by itself; when used singly, we see at once the meaning produced in a picture. But when both conventions are combined in one picture, puzzling and "impos-

DRAWING using at least three different spatial concepts. (1) Natural ("up is higher"), approach is combined with (2) Renaissance horizon line perspective in which "higher" can be level or even lower in the picture, and (3) space is "bent" in a way impossible in reality but possible on a flat surface. Viewing conventions combined despite the different conventions of viewing of each. (Drawing by the author, somewhat simplified, after an idea of the artist M. C. Escher in his drawing "Waterfall" in *The Graphic Work of M. C. Escher*, New York: Ballantine Books paperback, 1971, Plate No. 76.).

# Beasts and Battles

sible" visual effects can be produced. Such productions are "unfair" logically, but are nevertheless fun to view. (The so-called "primitive" school of art is yet something else, and may contain elements of both "perspective" and "natural" approaches.).

There is some similarity between the use of words to point in several directions at once and the use of different artistic conventions or approaches simultaneously which are normally not found together. Both seem to be logical tricks.

There is a further way to view spatial elements in an artist's work. The modern artist Hans Hofmann, now deceased, wished to discard the "perspective" view of the picture, and use just the psychological nature of the colors to create "depth" in paintings. In that view, the warm colors such as red, orange, and yellow seem to "advance" toward the eye; they "move nearer" to the viewer. The cold or cooler colors tend to "recede" from the eye; blues may "retreat" from the eye, thus creating "space" in the picture (called by Hofmann the "picture plane"). According to that view, it is not logical to use perspective approaches to the paper or canvas, and such approaches would be artificial. Since the picture surface is flat (flat canvas, or flat paper), it is not logical to attempt to produce an illusion of three dimensions on something that is two-dimensional like the canvas. But if "warm" colors advance and "cool" colors recede, then the artist could produce his "space" in the picture *simply by juxtaposing the colors of the paint*; the psychological effect of "movement" of such colors would create a "space" or "depth" logically in keeping with the surface being worked on by the artist. In that view, even perspective illusion would be a misuse of logic, and a sort of "trick" or logical fraud. But that is more a matter of philosophical difference, and not a logical trick of the type we have been considering, in which completely different approaches are mixed in together to create a puzzle. Or when words are used in ways that seem logical, but are not.

Puzzles can be fun, and some are capable of being solved, or at least understood, if one considers how they are made. Their structure can be a key to understanding. Sometimes we need to get past the surface presentation of the puzzle, and observe its key elements; and our reward may be an insight into something that doesn't make much sense on the surface—but yet seems as though it did.

# ▶ 8 ◀

# THE WESTERN DRAGON

Our ancestors believed in dragons. They had "proof" of a kind, for sometimes they might have information of giant bones found—perhaps of whales, extinct elephants, or even dinosaurs. One must smile at the tale of the atheist in the ancient world, who dug up a "sacred" grave out of curiosity, found some very large bones (perhaps of whale) in the ground, and immediately became religiously inclined.

The form that is in medieval stories is quite peculiar. Many animals are large and dangerous, some fly, and none at all have any ability to breathe fire as a weapon. Pre-cooked meals are not part of the general scheme of nature in the animal world. When the great scaly shape appears in literature of the past, we may be at a loss to explain it. We cannot relate it to what we know, and are left to simply wonder at human imagination.

Not everything in the past that is recorded is based upon something real, but some things are. In this chapter, we will attempt to show that the Western Dragon may have been real.

A classic description of the western "dragon" is found in the Old English heroic poem *Beowulf*. This dragon can fly, breathe fire, and carries poison. It sleeps in an old stone tower, and when someone penetrates to the treasure hidden there, it wakes to launch out over the countryside to take vengeance. It must be confronted by the hero-king Beowulf, who kills it but dies of its poison.

Could the dragon described in *Beowulf* (tr. by Raffel, 1963), be a war-ship of the Byzantine Empire equipped with Greek Fire? If so, it would be a case of a legendary beast being based upon an inanimate object—a curious origin of at least some attributes of the dragon in western lore. As to flight, a ship in the poem itself is pictured as having bird-like characteristics, perhaps suggested by its sail:

"The ship foamed through the sea like a bird"

—*Op. cit.*, p. 30, line 218.

There are other things about the dragon that at least do not conflict with the idea of a ship. Its length of fifty feet (*op. cit.*, p. 117) is fairly small for an ancient war-ship (see Frost, Honor: "How Carthage Lost the Sea", article in *Natural History* magazine, Dec., 1987, for suggestive information on sizes of war-ships in much earlier Roman times, esp. p. 67). Yet it is true that in an emergency any ships at hand were used by Constantinople for defense (cf. Psellus, *Fourteen Byzantine Rulers*, tr. Sewter, 1984, p. 201); and it is also true that the poet of *Beowulf* doubtless understood the "dragon" to be a beast—whose length he kept believable. In his very interesting book *The Hill of the Dragon* (1979), Paul Newman has no reference to the idea that the dragon itself was sometimes a ship of the Eastern Roman Empire (Byzantine Empire), and so is not responsible for the contention put forward here. His work does make some connection of dragons to Vikings, among many other and varied references.

In several places Newman refers to dragons as having a certain number of "iron teeth" (*op. cit.*, pp. 118, 141). This may be taken by us to refer to a ship's crew, given the Norse love of metaphor: x number of iron teeth equating to x number of swords—therefore x number of warriors on a ship.

Some stories and even legends of the past may point to a factual core. It does seem likely that the crocodiles of the Nile and the pythons of Africa have contributed elements to the northern people's ideas of "dragons". A "dragon" could have disparate elements. Though it is difficult of proof, when one adds the Greek Fire war-ship to the "creatures" found in the south, one seems to have elements that—dimmed by time and distance—could lead to such an odd creature as the western world's legendary "dragon". The contention here is not that all legends have a factual core or origin, but that in certain cases such a meaning may be found; in this regard one might mention the idea that the northern

# The Western Dragon

god Odin's eight-legged horse could refer to pall-bearers at a funeral (a plausible contention of H. R. Ellis Davidson in her *Gods and Myths of Northern Europe*, 1984, pp. 142-143). We will not here deal with the nature of the hero Beowulf, except insofar as his epic refers to the ancient Geats, other Swedes, and Danes.

That the Greek root for "dragon" means "snake" or "serpent" is interesting when compared to such Norse names for their own ships as "Long Serpent"; there is, of course, the usage "dragon ship", which in a simple way brings our attention to the contention put forward in this paper. Though there may be a good deal of coincidence in these names and terms, they are suggestive.

Beowulf was supposedly a Geat from the south of Sweden (Raffel, pp. 29, 137, 138), and the part played by Swedes in settling areas of Russia along trade routes leading eventually to Byzantium (Constantinople) is well known historically. We will mention later some links from Sweden to southeastern England which are again suggestive, though they point to a time prior to the probable time of composition of the *Beowulf* epic.

In the ancient poem, the hero Beowulf goes to Denmark and has adventures of a novel sort against monsters (one of which, called "Grendel", almost seems a "Bigfoot" candidate, and very hostile). Beowulf's last adventure is against the fierce dragon guarding its tower treasures. It is interesting (though perhaps another coincidence), that these adventures take place in Denmark, and some centuries later the "Danelaw" is officially established in England. The Danes were there before that time, so there is potential connection for the passage of real historical information in a garbled form. Thus we have a rough connection between Sweden through Russia to Byzantium/Constantinople; and from Sweden to Denmark and from Denmark to England—in real historical context. There are other links for the passage of information and tales, as we shall show later.

In the Norse tales of the "Twilight of the Gods", *fire is associated with the south* (cf. *New LaRousse Enclopedia of Mythology*, 1968, p. 276), from which direction fire will be brought against the gods. Whether the dangerous southern forces represent Greek Fire, volcanoes, or something else probably cannot be determined.

It is true that a fire that could be directed, and that water could not extinguish, must have made a deep impression upon those who became aware of it. In the *Alexiad* of Anna Comnena

# Beasts and Battles

(tr. Sewter, 1985, pp. 360-362), there is a description of the use of Greek Fire at the end of the 11th century: bronze or iron beast heads covered with gold were put on ship's prows, and there was a mechanism to move a tube (projecting from the beasts' mouths), up and down and side to side, so that the Greek Fire could be directed as a sort of naval flame thrower.

Psellus (*op. cit.*, pp. 201-202) relates the victory over Prince Vladimir's fleet in the mid 11th century. Over a hundred years earlier the same weapon had held off Prince Igor's fleet (Jones, *A History of the Vikings*, 1984, p. 260). Some sort of siphon mechanism seems to have been used in the Greek Fire weapon, as noted by Guerdan (*Byzantium*, tr. Hartley, 1962, p. 119). Clearly the fire weapon may have been used earlier than in defense against the major attacks noted above, since it was *invented in the latter part of the 7th century* (Sewter gives a date of about 673 A.D. in Appendix I of his translation of the *Alexiad*). The actual mechanism and the composition of the fuel for Greek Fire remained a secret of state for centuries, and its "napalm" type composition is not known even now as to its exact nature—though there have been some modern attempts at reconstruction of the secret. In the 9th century the Moors of Spain used their own version of the weapon, their naphtha setting some Viking raiding ships afire (Jones, *op. cit.*, p. 214).

The people Beowulf leads and the setting of the epic both refer to a time earlier than the invention of the Greek Fire; one of the kings or chieftains mentioned in the poem lived in the 6th century (Raffel, p. 141). The poem itself may well incorporate much older material. There is considerable support for a date of composition in the 8th century (cf. Raffel, p. xi of Introduction). A more flexible time, but still centering on the 8th century is provided by Peter Hunter Blair, *Roman Britain and Early England 55 B.C.–A.D. 871*, 1966, p. 20; he gives 650 A.D. through 850 A.D. Michael Wood, in his useful survey *In Search of the Dark Ages*, 1987, p. 88, presents the 8th century as time of composition (his book is not be be confused with Hollywood television shows). If the epic was composed in the 8th century, then we have a very nice fit chronologically with the invention of Greek Fire in the last part of the 7th century; and not too great a time will have elapsed since the 6th century setting contained in the poem.

How could material representing a state of society in Swe-

# The Western Dragon

den's 6th century be preserved long enough to be found in an epic composed in the 8th century? Even if 8th century kingships were considerably similar to the older societies in their interest in heroic poetry? It is generally agreed that Homer's *Iliad* preserves material from an earlier bronze age society, transmitted orally by court singers (or public singers; cf. later medieval bards and troubadors). The *Beowulf* was presumably composed in England, and the Anglo-Saxons at the time of its origin in either the early or the late 8th century were the inheritors of a bardic tradition that preserved older material orally (cf. Blair, *op. cit.*, p. 16). These bards could well have preserved the older material coming from the 6th and (if they had heard early of the Greek Fire), 7th centuries. If it was written down in the 8th century, the time covered is not so great. If it was written down in a later century, however unlikely that may be, the case of the *Iliad* shows such lengthy preservation of ancient material to be at least conceivable.

There is an element of the "dragon" that seems to be based on the crocodile. In an English church one such is pictured eating a man (Newman, *op. .cit.*, p. 156). Oddly enough, this intrusion of crocodiles as dragons may lead us back again to Byzantium—in the various stories of the "dragons led on a leash." Several instances are given by Newman (*op. cit.*, pp. 50-51, 52, 154-156) of Christian Saints or holy people "taming" dragons and leading them away like pet dogs. This does seem very strange, but now we notice a description of events in the amphitheatre at Byzantium/Constantinople as related by René Guerdan (*op. cit.*, p. 62):

"There were exhibitions of strange animals and acrobatic feats. Clowns performed and dwarfs waddled about. Animal tamers paraded gilded crocodiles on leads."

Is a real event to be linked to a later tale? In any case, here seems a possible origin of a colorful tale, whether in reality or in a traveller's or chronicle-writer's invention.

The Emperors of the Eastern Roman Empire in Byzantium surrounded themselves with a Varangian Guard, as the earlier Emperors of Italian Rome had made use of the Praetorian Guard. In Byzantium, the "Varangians" could be composed of Scandinavians, Germans, Russians, and even Englishmen and Danes after

# Beasts and Battles

the Norman conquest (Jones, *op. cit.*, p. 266). As Erik Wahlgren, in *The Vikings and America*, 1986, p. 35, puts it:

"Swedes served along with Danes and Norwegians in the so-called Varangian Guard of the Eastern Emperor at Byzantium, and were handomely rewarded for it."

Clearly, some of these men would later have returned to the north, thus providing one pathway for knowledge of events in the south. Northerners were also employed on campaign in the field, as was Harald—failed invader of England in 1066 A.D. Employment was well paid (Guerdan, *op. cit.*, p. 109, writes that the troops were the "best paid in the world"). Byzantium was in fact the richest city in the western world—a place any Viking would dearly love to plunder. It was in effect a huge "pot of gold". And it guarded many ancient treasures, as did the dragon in his tower in *Beowulf.*
    European forces out to carve out little kingdoms of their own and gain booty (they had to have that to pay their troops), continually fought the forces of the Byzantines. On Crusade they made war on the Byzantines as well as against "Saracens"; in 1203 A.D. the attacking French encountered Englishmen and Danes defending Constantinople (Villehardouin, *Chronicle*, tr. Shaw, pp. 70, 74).
    Earlier we saw Beowulf's ship compared to a bird. The Roman poet Horace seems to have had a similar idea in his poem praising the Roman Emperor's peaceful protection (cf. *The Complete Works of Horace*, Modern Library ed., p. 281). We next will note an even more interesting quotation from Snorri Sturluson's *King Harald's Saga, (Heimskringla)*, p. 109:

"Men will quake with terror
Before the seventy sea-oars

    . . .

Norwegian arms are driving
This iron-studded dragon
Down the storm-tossed river
Like an eagle with wings flapping."
                    (tr. by Magnus Magnusson and Hermann Pálsson).

Here the ship is both a bird and a dragon; it does everything except breathe fire. The links to ships seem evident. The link to birds seems at first sight to be more difficult, but we have seen already

# The Western Dragon

three times where poets have used such a metaphor; it seems fairly common. It should be noted that Sir Arthur Evans should receive credit for noticing that a ship's sails might be seen as bird's wings, in a letter of August, 1900 to a London newspaper:

"Here Daedalus constructed the Labyrinth, the den of the Minotaur, and fashioned the *wings—perhaps the sails* (my stress, h.t.)—with which he and Icarus took flight over the Aegean . . . "

—from Leonard Cottrell's *The Bull of Minos*, 1968, p. 118.

A ship could fly, but only the Byzantine war-ship could both fly and breathe fire. And that fleet guarded a very large treasure. (A small point aside here: one wonders if this was the "Rome" that some Vikings yearned to conquer; the Italian Rome had long since fallen in their time, and we know that the citizens of Constantinople sometimes called themselves "Romans", though the Greek language had at last gained precedence. They had, after all, inherited the eastern part of the old Empire. The Eastern Roman Empire did not fall until 1453 A.D. if one discounts the temporary Crusader occupation of the capital city.) Byzantium was by far the most tempting target for attack and looting, though its walls and its fire-ships were strong enough to repel invaders for a very long time.

The hero *Beowulf* was mortally wounded not by the dragon's fire, but had died of its poison. How could a ship inject poison? In point of fact, more people expire from *smoke inhalation* than are actually burned to death in fires. Can that be the secret of the dragon's "poison"?

All the elements mentioned so far as chief parts of the dragon are found far to the south of Scandinavia: the python, the crocodile, and the Byzantine warship carrying Greek Fire. The dragon, it is here contended, is not one creature. It is sometimes one thing and sometimes another, and sometimes perhaps a composite. These different features are clearly seen in Newman's *The Hill of the Dragon*. There we see psychological factors and various physical descriptions from the dragon lore.

According to the ideas presented in this paper, we now take the view that one of the dragon's historic elements may be *an inanimate object*. And this inanimate object is based directly

# Beasts and Battles

in historic reality. This does not preclude additional approaches to the subject from the standpoints of anthropology and psychology, but those approaches are for the most part outside the direction of thought presented here.

Another pointer to the Byzantine Empire may be the story of Saint George and the Dragon. This story is located in the Byzantine Empire or its adjacent area, whether or not the story has any basis in fact. It is mentioned here only in order to highlight yet another clue as to the general location of the "dragon". Whether from Palestine or near-by, St. George is from a sphere of influence of the Eastern Roman (Byzantine) Empire.

It is likely that the stories of the dragon would have moved north along the Russian trade routes between Constantinople and Scandinavia. Furs would come south, and certainly information would flow north along with Byzantine exports. The Swedes and other northerners would become absorbed in the Slavic population along the trade route settlements, but the trade routes would continue to exist in those places as well as in other directions. As Jones states (*op. cit.*, p. 259):

"With their contribution to the ever-grinding mill of Byzantine trade, the Rus were welcome, even favoured, visitors, while politically it suited the emperor to have a khaganate at Kiev strong enough to restrain the turbulence of local tribes . . . "

While antagonistic toward the old "diffusionist" approach, Colin Renfrew in *Before Civilization: The Radiocarbon Revolution and Prehistoric Europe*, 1973, p. 249, admits some effect of influence from one place to another:

"Clearly the effects of culture contact must continue to play a major role in our thinking."

It seems possible, even probable, that stories about the Greek Fire weapon would flow north along the merchants' routes running through what was to become Russia. Other trade routes would lead through Italy into northern Europe; and the channels of state diplomacy and churchly communication would provide additional conduits for tales of the Greek Fire war-ship, and of course of the python and crocodile as well. And, at the end of the

# The Western Dragon

trade-routes, in Scandinavia and England, the bards would sing or recite the things of interest to the society.

It is not necessary for Beowulf himself to be a real historical character, though he may have been. Blair (*op. cit.*, p. 20), considers that he is fictitious and his adventures fabulous. But the epic points to at least one historical character of the 6th century (Raffel, *op. cit.*, pp. 137, 138, 141 in an "Afterword" by R. P. Creed). Beowulf's tribe actually existed (*ibid*, p. 138). Blair also believes that the people were real historically, and that the social setting is valuable historically (*op. cit.*, pp. 20-21).

If the *Beowulf* epic was composed at the court of the English King Offa of Mercia (cf. Wood, *op. cit.*, p. 88), this would take place in the last half of the 8th century. That would be somewhat more or somewhat less than one hundred years after the date of the invention of Greek Fire in the 670's A.D., and would be a good chronological fit for the distance between the event and the epic. It should be noted that London was a "Mercian" town (Wood, p. 121), and was a trading center in those days; it was active in overseas trade in the seventh and eighth centuries (Wood, p. 74).

The archaeological finds at Sutton Hoo in southeast England also show possible links between England and Sweden, and even to Constantinople (cf. Wood, pp. 64, 73, 74-75). These finds may be from a period too early for the composition of the epic, or even before the invention of Greek Fire; they nevertheless show interesting lines of communication for the possible later passage of information. There may have been many more smaller English coastal or near-coastal trading centers in the seventh and eighth centuries A.D. (cf. e.g. Wood, p. 74). And we should not ignore the possible role of York to the north.

Daniel Cohen (*A Modern Look at Monsters*, 1970, p. 42), wrote that the dragon's bulk was based on the python in his opinion, and its fiery breath probably on the poisonous nature of smaller snakes. The contention in this paper is, however, that *the fire of the dragon is not a symbolic fire, but is real fire.* But the python does seem to come into the subject, from Scandinavian rock carvings and from the accounts in Newman's interesting book.

In depicting the dragon (and other animals), the Norwegians seem to have been influenced by the art styles of Irish illuminated manuscripts (cf. the article "The Stave Churches of Norway", in *Scientific American*, August, 1983, esp. p. 99 and caption to the

**93**

# Beasts and Battles

illustration on p. 102). Such material may have come into their hands as a result of raids. In this connection, it is important to draw a distinction between how something is depicted, and *why one would want to depict it at all.* It is possible that the motivation here is the Viking respect for a noteworthy weapon of war, transformed into elements of a hero's great battle against a terrible animal adversary. One can well argue that the accounts of a weapon strong enough to be seen as a sort of "ultimate weapon" by some of the people of the time (much as gunpowder was regarded in a later era), would become widespread. Such accounts of real events would become garbled and changed to some extent in travelling from the Mediterranean and Black Sea areas to the peoples of the north. Some accounts would pass through the Balkans toward the north, and from the German peoples to the Scandinavians. In the passing, some accounts may have been transformed from tales of naval actions to tales of land animals. The bards who sang of the deeds of heroes to the Scandinavians and Anglo-Saxon English were not at the scene of the action even if the things sung or recited stemmed from real events originally. They were at the end of a lengthy geographical chain of communication, and in addition, the things recited would likely not be understood simply by virtue of the passage down the years from one narrator to another.

Again, we note that the Scandinavians and the Anglo-Saxons thought of the dragon as an animal, not as a ship. The "dragon" in the Anglo-Saxon *Beowulf* tale is an animal, though it lives beside the sea (as Constantinople is also located by the Black Sea and Sea of Marmora: another pointer to Byzantium?). The "dragon" as depicted in rock carvings seems to be more like a python than anything else, and is the land creature that Sigurd stabs (compare the German Sigfried). Thus, in the rock carvings and legends, the dragon has become a land creature. And the Vikings would very likely have known of the python first hand from their raids in the south, their military service there, and their trade with the area. (The carvings on rocks present a curious puzzle: the pythonesque "dragon" in these carvings seems to always have some sort of "fringe" or "gill structure" near its head—yet the presumption is that a land creature is meant to be portrayed.)

The fire of the dragon was not, if these ideas of Byzantine origin are correct, derived from the color of a creature's tongue as drawn and painted in illuminated manuscripts—although such depictions may have influenced how the Scandinavian artists made their portrayals. The contention here is that the dragon was, in its "final" *Beowulf* form, derived from a ship that was firmly based in history.

The Romans may have used animal devices (cf. the "eagles"). The post-Roman Britons may or may not have used the dragon as a device on a banner which might "fly" in the wind. But it is doubtful whether these devices ever spouted fire.

The dragon was too good a stock character to leave out of a story in the medieval world. One is found on land in a wood in the account of Yvain (Chrétien de Troyes, *Yvain, the Knight of the Lion*, tr. by Raffel, 1987, p. 101); that dragon had the ability to breathe out fire. In many of the Arthurian tales, the dragon retains its role of the dutiful guardian of treasure; and in Scandinavian tales serpents guard a "netherworld" type of place, perhaps in reference to graves and treasures buried with the dead (cf. Davidson, *op. cit.*, pp. 139, 159-162).

But the idea of a fire-breathing serpent (at least one type of "basilisk"), was more than six or seven hundred years earlier than the Byzantine invention. How are we to account for these early Roman views? We have the same problem with other early "creatures", such as the bull that Jason had to harness in his quest for the Golden Fleece. How could any animal spout fire? It is conceivable that some ancient statues were hollow, and that fires could be kindled within them. The Phoenicians and Carthaginians performed human sacrifices, but their statues were not serpentine, so far as we know.

Could a person's fever resulting from snakebite be taken as a sign that the serpent's breath was "fiery" (in the sense of everything being divided into air, earth, water, or fire)? Such an explanation seems far too forced.

Moses' serpent image made in the desert to fend off other snakes, and the large serpent at Athena's feet in the Athenian Parthenon show that large images of snakes were made.

We really have no explanation, but will make one speculation. In the April, 1988 copy of the magazine *Natural History*, there is a letter of explanation from a scholar as to why a tiger is shown on a Carthaginian mosaic (there normally being no tigers in Africa). The reason given—the tiger was copied from an artist's

# Beasts and Battles

Syrian sketchbook—provides a potential explanation of fire-mouthed snakes: the forked and red tongues being mistaken for flames. We have no better explanation. Meantime, we will show more communication links to Byzantium.

There are apparent trade-routes through what was later to become France, Belgium, and Holland. The glass wares produced in Roman times were still being made and exported during the 6th century from north Francia to Anglo-Saxon England and Scandinavia (James, *The Franks*, 1988, pp. 202-203). Later the Franks made and traded the best swords (James, pp. 203-204), which the English and Scandinavians would certainly appreciate. Wealthy Frankish women wore Byzantine ear-rings or imitations of them in the time of Charlemagne and just before (8th and 9th centuries), as James has stated (James, p. 226). Byzantine gold-embroidered silks were available for Frankish aristocrats.

It may seem incongruous for Scandinavians or English well north of Byzantium to know of events in that place before the real beginning of the so-called "Viking Age" of roughly 793-1100 A.D. But about 375 A.D., a long time before that age, they knew of the defeat of the Gothic kingdom at the Black Sea by the Huns. Scandinavians incorporated that event in the songs or recitations of their bards (Derry, *A History of Scandinavia*, 1979, p. 10).

If one trade route was blocked, it can be seen that there were other paths through which information could pass to the north, while amber, furs, and slaves passed to the south. There will also have been trade with the Arabs. No one path for news was vital, for there were always others, such as the German millstone trade route from the Rhine to Gaul and England (James, p. 203). Archaeology and history show many links between southern and northern peoples in the early medieval period, and clearly these paths provide possible conduits for the passage of knowledge and gossip.

A recounting of some of these lines of communication may seem tedious. Those mentioned should be considered as only part of a network that existed during the early medieval period, whose sections might shorten or lengthen or change altogether in places. But they demonstrate that many areas of the medieval world were not isolated from news or information of events transpiring elsewhere. Very late channels of information and very early ones should be considered in connection with the passage of "dragon"

# The Western Dragon

information. The early channels or routes show the possibilities of later transmission of information, as they might still be in place at a later date. The very late channels should still be noted, in the event that the composition of the *Beowulf* epic took place later than we suppose (or, if added, that the "dragon" motif was added to an extant epic at a later time). Aristocrats and kings would not have been as isolated and cut off from the world around them as would the average man or woman, and it was in those circles that heroic epics and poetry would circulate.

The ancient use of words such as "orm" and "worm" suggest very strongly a snake-like shape for a dragon. The medieval literary hero Gawain encounters dragons in British forests in the story of "Gawain and the Green Knight", and the old Anglo-Saxon word for "dragon" may be "worm" (see for instance Richard Barber's *King Arthur: Hero and Legend*, 1986, p. 109, "wormes" fought by Gawain). And the British tales of the warriors that use armor with outward projecting spikes against dragons seem to show an interesting idea for defense against very large constrictor type creatures. And it is the python type that is clearly featured in the ancient world's Laocoön statue.

Two dragons had come from the sea to punish Laocoön and his sons as well, sent by the gods. While the python is depicted in the carving, the fact that the creatures had come from water seems to point to the crocodile somewhat more than to a snake—at least insofar as the verbal legend is concerned. (While it is true that pythons swim, it is also true that maidens set out as sacrifices for "dragons" could not be eaten by pythons while chained or tied to post or rock. And, since crocodiles prefer soft rotting flesh, staked out captives would be more likely to be mauled by them than "eaten". But perhaps we should ignore the legends such as that of "Perseus frees the maiden"; after all, neither pythons nor crocodiles were found near Troy, Laocoön's location. We note the tales as pointers to early human sacrifice, and pass on—with a final comment that pythons do not group together.)

Mercenaries who served the Byzantine Empire may or may not have heard old wine-shop tales of Herakles and the dragon, or of Perseus or Jason or Laocoön; but they very likely would have heard of the fire-throwing war-ships, and perhaps of the python and the crocodile (the last a known man-eater in Africa). The Sumero-Babylonian dragon was of another age.

# Beasts and Battles

There were other mercenaries serving in France (what was to later become France, at any rate). In the event that the final encounter of the hero with the dragon is a later addition to the already extant "Beowulf" story, there is a very simple possible connection between Saxon areas of England (where it seems the epic was preserved and eventually written down in the eighth century), and ports of southern France into which the fiery war-ship tales could enter. Some of the mercenaries that served in southern France were Saxons.

In the fifth century the coast of France was troubled by Saxon pirates; these "had established themselves at the mouth of the Garonne as well as the Loire" (cf. Herwig Wolfram's *History of the Goths*, 1988, pp. 174, 190, and esp. p. 237). The pirates were sea-going, of course, and the Gothic power of south-western France authorized a fleet manned by pre-Gothic inhabitants to be used against them (Wolfram, pp. 174, 190). And, though these Saxons were pirates, they may also have engaged in smuggling as well, or at least had access to some of the ports of England. Some of their descendants (or some new group of Saxons) were in southern France in the seventh century, *at perhaps the exact date that Greek Fire was first used in 673 A.D.*, (see Wolfram, p. 237, for this). Here history may be added to archaeological evidence of trade-routs, and shows what may have been the obvious "news channel" for word of the advent of the "fire-breathing ships". We know that Marseilles was engaged in international trade, and received shipments of, e.g., oil (cf. James, *op. cit.*, p. 206, using Gregory of Tours as a source; most of James' book, however, is based upon archaeological evidence). Greece was a producer of olive oil, and a part of the Byzantine empire. And, earlier, in the late 6th century, Greeks were " . . . active in long-distance trading and in the money business" (Wolfram, *op. cit.*, p. 234). The Franks and the Visigoths who hired the Saxon troops in France (Wolfram, pp. 237, 238) certainly knew the Byzantines as a dangerous power, since in the 6th century Byzantine armies had campaigned in Italy and destroyed the Ostrogothic kingdom there; somewhat later they also crushed Frankish forces that attempted to take a role in Italian conflicts.

Some of the "routes of rumor;" that archaeology and history have shown will have been blocked, some will have been too early and ceased at the relevant times, and some too late for the passage of news events of the Greek Fire ships to the north of Europe—and subsequent use in the bardic constructions finally written down as the epic *Beowulf*. But we have seen so many ways for the passage of news that we may safely say: there was a real fire-breathing ship, and there were numerous ways that news of this development could reach the north and England. The archaeological evidence for ancient trade-routes and the remnants of history left from the Dark Ages support the contention to such an extent that it becomes even probable that the fiery dragon of the *Beowulf* poem was in fact based as we have shown insofar as its "flight" and "fire" are concerned (and perhaps also its concern to punish those who raided its territory).

The "treasure" that the dragon guarded was very important. Wolfram has shown that treasure was emblematic of kingship (pp. 205-206, 220, 221, 351, 361; on p. 469, note 412, he cites Jordanes, *Getica*, 215-218, p. 113, for the "notion that the treasure, the capital, and the kingdom are one and the same."). From this one might infer that the dragon was in fact a representation of a king, but we have shown otherwise—it seems to have been representative of the guardian of a king.

We have at least three broad ways for tales of the ships with Greek Fire to reach the northern peoples: northerners who raided the south and sometimes soldiered in it, trade routes, and the communication of a diplomatic nature between governments and church powers.

That the dragon that spat fire was not more directly and clearly understood was a product of the difficulties in communication over time and distance in the medieval world. Added to these difficulties were the differences in religion and culture generally between the Latin Catholics and their followers and allies, and the Greek Christians of Constantinople. A great gulf of attitude separated those peoples, and this often eventuated in hostilities. After all, the passages cited earlier in which Anna Comnena described the use of Greek Fire on the prows of Byzantine ships were in the context of use against Latin Catholic Christians.

# ◆ 9 ◆

# MEDUSA AND FRIENDS

Some mysteries, though not all, have a fairly simple explanation. Such explanations may be disappointing. They can give one a real "let-down" feeling. Professional magicians very wisely keep their illusions and tricks a secret because of this fact of human nature, and to protect their livelihood. And, as L. Sprague de Camp has noted, people will spend a lot to be deceived, but very little to be enlightened (in L. S. de Camp, *The Fringe of the Unknown*, Prometheus Press, 1983 paperback, p. 170).

Nevertheless, sometimes the seemingly incomprehensible can be understood easily when additional information is available. A case in point comes from World War II. Nearing the end of the war, there was mounting evidence that something was going on in the Ardennes. There were increasing signs of German activity, despite the German effort to maintain strict secrecy. Yet allied headquarters ignored these signs, until the German offensive creating the Battle of the Bulge burst upon them. How could the buildup of entire armies be ignored? When you know that the allied high command was reading the German code machine (which normally detailed their intentions), and that the Germans *had not used* that machine for this offensive—then there is no longer a mystery. The Germans had used couriers to hand-carry orders and messages (noted in John Toland's book *Battle: The Story of the Bulge*, Signet Books, 1959 paperback, pp. 24-25). The code machine being secretly read by the allies had no mention of the operation, and therefore no one with command authority was about to believe in a secret attack.

## Beasts and Battles

Some make a mystery of watches that have stopped running but "miraculously" begin to work again because of "psychic power". Sometimes watches may stop running because their interior oil has cooled and "gummed up" the works. The magician James ("The Amazing") Randi has pointed out that the heat of the hand and a little shaking can make many watches begin running again. It is known that heat thins oil, while cold thickens it. This being so, anyone attempting to start their watch by "concentration" should allow time for the heat of their hand to warm the watch-case.

Clearly the subject of "strange phenomena" includes evidence affected by hoax (seeking publicity), and fiction, (seeking to entertain), so that the evidence itself is likely to be a problem for anyone wishing to take certain claims seriously in order to draw conclusions from them. When investigations are made of some claims, the evidence seems to vanish. That may be the case with a strange story in the Frank Edwards book *Stranger Than Science*, (Citadel Press; Secaucus, N.J.; no date; see Chapter 1, "The Mystery of David Lang", p. 15, paperback ed.). A Tennessee farmer is said to have vanished in plain sight of his wife and a friend while walking across a field. He was never found, and in the spot of his disappearance, a round patch of "stunted" amber grass was found; months later his children heard his faint cry for help, which faded away.

Nickell and Fischer, in *Secrets of the Supernatural*, (Prometheus Books; Buffalo, N.Y.; 1988), have shown in convincing fashion that this story is invented (not by Mr. Edwards, however; see Chapter 5, p. 61 and ff. of Nickell and Fischer). The same inventiveness may hold for another tale repeated by Edwards, "The Disappearance of Oliver Larch", in *Strangest of All*, (Citadel Press; Secaucus, N.J.; p. 119 of paperback ed.). Nickell and Fischer make a good case that these tales, which were doubtless published in good faith by Edwards in the 1950's, were in fact hoaxes and "copycat" stories that may go back to stories of like nature from the works of the writer Ambrose Bierce. This author (who himself disappeared, either in Mexico or somewhere along the Colorado River—perhaps intentionally), is noted as the possible founder of "spin-offs" from his popular fiction; Nickell and Fischer are likely to be correct in this view.

Ambrose Bierce would not have been alone in being inter-

# Medusa and Friends

ested in ideas such as that of a "door" to another dimension. One thinks of the old classic fairy stories. Later, when Einstein first made an impact with his new ideas, people could talk of the "fourth dimension". We know this to have been an error: Einstein viewed Time itself as the fourth dimension, in addition to the usual ones of height, depth, and breadth. (So now writers must go on to the fifth or more dimensions, if they wish to use these ideas—though our physicists with the "Superstrings" are monopolizing such thoughts nowadays, with their concepts of very tiny dimensions.)

If Nickell and Fischer are right, and a travelling salesman put forth the tale of the disappearing farmer, then we cannot link this tale to such topics as the "Bermuda Triangle" or "Flying Saucers". These authors, in the same work, show reason to believe that the "moving coffins" in a sealed vault type of story is also a spin-off of an earlier odd story, or invented for other reasons; they believe that the event on the island of Barbados is fictitious (see Chapter 10 of *Secrets of the Supernatural*, especially p. 147). Some earlier event may have caused such a tale to be spread; somewhere ground-water may have risen in a closed vault and floated coffins into new positions, creating a puzzle. In any event, it seems the tale was good enough to keep repeating. Some oddities might be explained simply, while others remain forever a puzzle.

A hippopotamus may not look much like a horse to a modern American, yet the ancient Greeks called him "river horse". The Indian rhinocerous is not an exact replica of a horse either, but many writers have believed that the unicorn is based on that animal. The unicorn is supposed to be a horse with a single protruding horn in his forehead. We know that Alexander the Great took an army of many thousands through India in the fourth century B.C., and that tales of exotic creatures reached the West in that fashion—if not later through Roman trade communications. As the Greek word "hippopotamus" means "river horse", so it is easy to see that a rhinocerous might come to be transfigured into a medieval creature called the "unicorn" (or one-horn).

Some curiosities in old writers seem to be based on quite simple things. We know that people continually like to give animals human attributes and personalities; thus such descriptions as "dog-faced men" seem to point to baboons. And, to those of us with a simple mind, it may be that the Arabic giant "roc" is simply

REPRESENTATION of a goddess or priestess excavated at Knossos, major city of the pre-Hellenic Minoan civilization. If Medusa "turned men to stone", this might refer to "rigor mortis"—perhaps she presided over a cult which included human sacrifice? (Drawing by the author after a photograph in Peter Green's *Ancient Greece, An Illustrated History*, New York, Thames and Hudson, 1987 paperback, p. 31.) It is likely that the prehistoric civilization of Crete influenced early Greece in many ways.

# Medusa and Friends

the result of a story about the ostrich, writ large; we can ignore the extinct Madagascan "elephant bird".

To medieval Europeans, there was a creature that was "king" of the snakes: the "cockatrice". He had something odd about his head (a "crest, or comb" according to *Bulfinch's Mythology*, Modern Library, New York, no date, p. 250). He "advances lofty and upright"; could this be a cobra? We know that cobras rear upward with the fore-part of their length. The "weasel" was thought to be the "enemy" of the cocatrice, according to Bulfinch, (p. 251). Those of us who have read Kipling's stories of India would recognize the mongoose as this "weasel". The cockatrice was born from an egg in the nest of a toad or serpent (Bulfinch, p. 250); king cobras come from eggs. Like ghosts of the night, the cocatrice would be affected by the crow of a cock: while the ghost would vanish as the daylight approached, the cockatrice would die as it heard the sound. Some ancient people thought this cockatrice was the same as the basilisk (a creature whose look meant instant death, like the effect of the face of the ancient Greek female monster, Medusa). These descriptions (in Bulfinch, pp. 250-251), appear to indicate cobras, and it seems a possibility that descriptions of the "king cobra" were brought back by Alexander the Great's men on their return from India.

The Greek Medusa was one of three Gorgons; the other two were Sthenno and Euryale. They lived over the "ocean" from the Greeks. Medusa's sisters were immortal, but she was not, (for we know that she was killed by Perseus). The Gorgon Medusa gave birth to Pegasus, the winged horse, and also to the demigod Chrysaor (who was born holding a golden sword). Both Chrysaor and Pegasus were born after Perseus cut off Medusa's head with the use of a mirror. The Gorgons lived near a border of night, with the "Hesperides". Hesiod described the Gorgons in his *Theogony* (see p. 32, *Hesiod and Theognis*, Penguin Books, 1986 paperback, translation by Dorothea Wender).

The people of the ancient classical world were not too clear on how contagion or poison worked, though they knew the effects. Bulfinch (p. 250) quotes the Roman poet Lucan to the effect that a basilisk's venom could climb up the shaft of a lance and flow into the body of a man using it, causing death. And Josephus in his *Jewish War* described a terrible plant that had to be uprooted in a certain peculiar and cautious way: a rope was tied to a dog, and then fastened to the plant; the dog would then be encouraged to pull the plant out of the ground, but the power of the plant would flow through the rope and destroy the hound. Some of this procedure resembles the gathering of the plant called "Mandrake" in medieval Europe.

Some poisons were thought to be so potent that they must be transported in a hollowed-out hoof of an ass or mule; this would be especially true of the water of the fearful River Styx. (Can this be one germ of the medieval concept of the "Universal Solvent"?) Basilisks must be hunted with the use of a mirror, even as Perseus armed himself to meet Medusa.

But the breath of some basilisks could actually burn shrubs. The ancient view that everything was composed of fire, earth, air, and water may be responsible for this—a man's fever might be likened to a product of a "fiery" origin. Whatever the origin of the belief, the breath of the basilisk was considered as dangerous as the sighting of it. Perseus' caution in using a mirror against Medusa was wise, since her face was death to look upon. Her head grew serpents instead of hair, and her look turned men to stone. This "look of death" was shared by the "basilisk", a terrible serpent believed to be the cause of instant death also. In this regard, it is interesting to remember that Aristotle's theory of vision was the opposite of that in our modern world; he believed that when a person perceived an object, something "went out" of the person's eyes and travelled to the object (while we believe that light is reflected off an object and travels to our eyes, which then use their ability to produce the image of the object). This belief of some inner quality leaping from the eye outward may be the ancient theoretical basis of the belief in the so-called "evil eye", which is said to still be maintained by some devout Catholics (after all, in the old beliefs in "possession", one was thought to "harbor" an evil entity; if one believed that something could "fly out of the eye towards another person",—in the best tradition of Aristotle's theory of vision—then even the looks of a "possessed" person might be deemed harmful). The story of the basilisk, which does not exist, and the tale of Medusa still affect the modern world in some places, it seems.

Many attempts have been made to "explain" Medusa, and they have not succeeded. It may be that Medusa is a product of human imagination, and cannot be explained. It is also possible

# Medusa and Friends

that there is a very simple explanation underlying the whole story: an explanation so simple that it has not yet occurred to anyone. It may be that Medusa's effect, which was said to be to turn men to "stone", is to be explained by the simple fact that she caused a well-known phenomenon in her victims. She caused them to have rigor mortis, the rigid effect known to follow after death. She was known to be dangerous. She killed people, and her victims "stiffined up" and in this way "turned to stone".

She may have been the priestess of an early religion. In fact, her likeness may have been discovered. Many people have seen the little statue from Crete with the bare-bosomed woman holding snakes in her out-stretched hands: perhaps an early statue of a "goddess of the animals", or perhaps a priestess of such a belief.

There are definite indications of early Greek human sacrifice. We know of the story of Agamemnon's sacrifice of his daughter Iphigenia in order to procure favorable winds for the fleet to sail to Troy to recover Helen. We have as yet not much evidence about this from Crete, and it is true that Crete is not "across the Ocean" from Greece, though it is across the Sea. (In a completely speculative thought, one wonders if the "three" Gargons might have been Isis of Egypt, Artemis of Ephesus, and a "Mistress of the Animals" in Crete?).

The son of Medusa, Chrysaor with the "golden sword", might well point to a priest with the terrible occupation of putting people to death in a ritual way. Some scholars believed that ancient Druids used a golden sickle to cut mistletoe in some sort of ritual. Pegasus, the winged horse, is innocent of all this; and, as a horse, is sacred to his father Poseidon (as are all horses).

We cannot really find the locations of the Gorgons; Hesiod's early descriptions from perhaps the eighth century and near the time of "Homer" are vague. It is not certain what is meant by a location on an ocean shore near "Night". And the Hesperides might tend apple trees across the ocean, but that tells us little, also.

We know that the northern Celts made human sacrifices, and we have read that in his campaign north of Macedonia, Alexander discovered such a thing, done by the peoples in the general area of the Danube River. And the Carthagenians continued the practice even as late as Roman times.

The Greeks stopped the practice of human sacrifice, but scholars deduce that it once existed from various hints. Their

# Beasts and Battles

mortal hero, Herakles (Hercules), raised to divinity and Olympic residence after fulfilling his earthly life, was said to have stopped the practice of it in Egypt. (This would not have been a Greek figure. The Greeks subsumed foreign gods and figures under their own like figures' nomenclature: thus the Phoenician god Melkart was Herakles or Herakles-Melkart to the Greeks; and the Indian Vishnu might become incorporated into Herakles in so far as Greeks were concerned. When the Greeks write that "Herakles" captured Troy once before the time of the Trojan War, we may have a reference to a war of Phoenicians or even Hittites with Trojans, and not a record of a conflict involving a Greek figure at all.)

The classical scholar Michael Grant has a story in his *Roman Myths* (Dorset Press, no town, 1984, pp. 48-51), wherein Hercules slays an "ogre" that lives in a cave on or near the Aventine Mount in Italy, thereby freeing the natives of their fear of being killed and having their heads publicly displayed by the "ogre". The interesting thing about this story is that though he lives in a cave and kills people, this "ogre" also breathes smoke and fire. In keeping with our previous train of thought, one wonders if the destruction of the ogre Cacus may mirror a putting down of Carthagenian rites in Italy, and their replacement by Greek culture and animal sacrifice? We do know that there were Greek cities in south Italy, whose culture eventually affected Romans and Etruscans; and we also know that the Carthaginian religion contained the practice of burning infant victims, perhaps in hollow statues. This idea is, of course, speculation and nothing more, and not found in Grant's work. The Greeks may have given themselves undue credit for the prohibition of human sacrifice in the lands bordering the Mediterranean Sea.

Eight hundred years ago, the Greek story-teller in the Roman world, Apuleius, described the goddess Isis as sprouting poisonous serpents rising from her hair (pp. 236-240, and especially p. 237 of *The Golden Ass*, Pocket Books Inc., New York, 1956 paperback, translation by Robert Graves). She also carried a dish of gold with an asp ready to strike on its handle (p. 238). It is not clear whether these snakes are considered to be alive, or are only decorative ornaments. The two that rise from the head of the goddess uphold a moon symbol. When she speaks, she says that the Athenians know her as Artemis and the Cretans know her as Dictynna

# Medusa and Friends

(p. 239). The author Apuleius was not a Christian, and may have worshipped this goddess; in any event, he makes her go on to claim that she is known by many names—and when she lists these, she incorporates such famous names as Juno, Aphrodite, and Proserpine (p. 239). Here we see the Greek (and Roman) tendency to see diverse and even foreign deities as the same as one well-known to themselves.

The identification of Isis of Egypt with Artemis and Dictynna is interesting, despite two cautions: first, that the worship of Isis had spread much further than Egypt in the Roman era, and even into Rome itself; and second, that many gods or goddesses might claim to be many of the others in order to seem more powerful or worthy of worship. (That is, their worshippers or priests might claim such status for them.)

Bulfinch's *Mythology* (p. 251) states that the dead bodies of basilisks (identified as the cockatrice by some), were hung up in Greek and Roman temples (and even in private homes), in order to keep away spiders or birds; if these reasons seem rather inadequate when one considers the aesthetics of dead cobras hanging about, the custom may point to very early rites of some sort. Temples mentioned in Bulfinch (p. 251) are those of Apollo and Diana. Diana is, of course, the Greek Artemis—who had a very large temple at Ephesus on the coast of Asia Minor, and was a well-known fertility figure. It would seem that sometimes the ancients associated serpents with her, although the bull is more likely to be her animal; some historians have lately decided that the many "breasts" of female fertility figures (goddesses) really represent multiple bulls' testicles: sort of a fertility "overkill". There is at least one Hittite shrine in Asia Minor that contains a fresco of a bull being led by the nose, and even a stone "horns of consecration" like those discovered by Sir Arthur Evans of Cretan exploration fame.

But the snake keeps appearing again and again in history, literature, art, and prehistory. The Egyptian high crown hats worn by the pharaohs displayed a rearing cobra head at the base. (We will presume that the story of Medusa did not begin when, in the reign of Queen Hatshepsut, practical jokers out to impress Greek tourists might have claimed that stone statues of people in Egypt were really people turned into stone by priestly or pharaonic magic.) There was a statue of Athena, the protective deity of Athens,

# Beasts and Battles

in her temple on the Acropolis; at her feet was a large serpent, perhaps representing some sort of male deity from an early age; though this serpent seems more pythonic than poisonous due to its size, it seems that we cannot escape from snakes, no matter where we turn. And the little statues from Crete with the women handling serpents really seem a good base for a Medusa belief that was handed down to people in later ages in confused form, earlier rites or religious practices having been forgotten.

The serpent has a beneficent aspect, as we know from the "caduceus" wand of Hermes/Mercury that is used today in a modern version symbolic of medical practice. Any large serpent was unlikely to be admitted to a place in the Parthenon with Athena unless it had been "domesticated" or made an ally. Some authorities believe that the ancient Cretans kept pet snakes in their homes; if so, these were surely not of a venomous nature.

The Athenian goddess wore the severed head of Medusa upon her person when she went to war: this connects her with the Gorgon. The head, even severed, had the power to immobilize people, and would have made Athena yet more terrible in war than her spear and physical abilities. Sometimes a decorative type of Medusa-head image is seen on representations of ancient breast-plates; worn on one's armor, it might have some sort of psychological effect of weakening one's opponent.

There are very few legendary figures which seem to fit neatly upon some realistic base. Before leaving the subject, we should mention the figure of the Centaur. A creature that was half man and half horse, lustful, and loving wine. This figure has been noted by many writers as referring to a horse-riding tribe of people as perceived historically by people of a tribe that was unfamiliar with domesticated horses or riding. This view seems very reasonable, and we will add it to our list of "explained creatures". The list is very short, and probably should remain so; we will stress only those resemblances which seem to fit. Most legends will remain obscure.

The study of history sometimes produces surprising bits of information. The Britishh general Montgomery, famous for his success at the Battle of El Alamein in World War II, wrote that he was using an idea of rotating troops in that battle; when some had fought hard for a time, he would pull them back and send in fresh men. Officers from England questioned this tactic, but, as Montgomery said, were assured by his supporters (and by the result of the battle, perhaps), that he knew what he was doing. But we find that the ancient Roman commanders did the same thing (Livy, *Rome and the Mediterranean*, Penguin Classics, pp. 199, 272); Livy recounts how the Gauls were defeated in this manner in his Book XXXV, Ch. 5, and also the Spanish Ligurians in his Book XXXVI, Ch. 38. The idea of replacing fatigued troops with fresh ones thus goes back to at least the beginnings of the second century B.C., and perhaps even earlier. Montgomery may have produced this idea himself, or may have been remembering the tactics of ancient warfare; whatever his source, it is clear that his critics had forgotten their military history.

There are some parallels in legend that are noticeable but do not lead us to any definite conclusion: such is the tale of King Arthur's achievement in possessing the sword "Excalibur". We notice the peculiarity of a sword that is set in stone, and can only be drawn out by the hero. And it is interesting that there is a story in Germanic legend (perhaps more specifically Gothic legend), that seems similar: the tale of Sigmund's sword named "Gram". The god Odin entered Sigmund's house during a feast, and pushed the sword deeply into a great tree that grew in the middle of Sigmund's house (see, for instance, D. A. MacKenzie's *German Myths and Legends*, Avenel Books, New York, 1985, p. 289). Only Sigmund could withdraw the "magic" (or at least superior), blade; it eventually descended to his son, the hero Sigurd—slayer of the dragon. If the "Excalibur" and the "Gram" stories are somehow linked, we note the irony of Saxon (Germanic) elements entering into the legend of the Briton, Arthur, deemed to be the Saxons' chief opponent.

And then there is the similarity of the king who sleeps in or under a mountain, who will yet rouse and come again when his people are in need of him. True of Arthur—but also true of a German king. These things are peculiar to us because in our time we hate the entire population of the "enemy"; it was not always so. In the ancient world, one might have allies among the tribes of the enemy peoples one fought; Julius Caesar recruited Gauls for allies in his conquest of Gaul, after all. But we cannot be sure what the resemblances indicate in the Arthurian tales, and so will pass on without attempting to force a meaning.

The British sword had two different fates. In one version,

# Beasts and Battles

it was given away as a gift in Sicily by King Richard Lionheart while on Crusade (a wise move to have a friend at a key point on his supply line). In the other version it was cast into the lake, and received by an emerging hand and arm.

There is another way to draw a sword from rock: a smith can receive crushed rock, extract the ore, and fabricate a sword. But smiths are not great warrior-heroes, and are not kings.

One final comment before we leave the realm of legend: could the Romans be the "little people" of fairy-tale and antique lore? All historical accounts stress the height of the northern peoples as opposed to the Romans; the Celtic warriors that went into battle naked except for neck torques and weapons were always described as much taller than the Romans who fought them. This suggestion is meant solely to go to the origin of the "size" question, and is independent of later accretions of attributes (with the possible exception of the warning not to get them angry: people that would crucify thousands were not to be trifled with).

This suggestion flies in the face of the current wisdom about incoming Celts meeting "small, dark Picts", but seems worth making anyway. Picts may have been smaller than Celts, but Romans were so small that Gauls, Germans, and other Celts laughed at them, until they demonstrated their discipline. References to the "good people" or "Gentry" (fairies) having some sort of "ever-burning light or lamp" might point to the Romans; there was an old story that three cities in the Roman Empire knew such a secret: Rome, Alexandria, and Antioch. Such a thing might seem impossible (and might be just a legend), but it may be possible that the ancients did know how to locate and channel gas from pockets of natural gas in the earth, or even perhaps use some sort of phosphorescent paint material as a lasting (dim) light. In addition to a possible connection with memories of the Roman legions or cavalry, old tales of a dwarfish race of bowmen might point to the followers of Atilla the Hun, whose progress through Europe was only stopped in France in the mid fifth century, and whose fame (or notoriety) spread completely over Christendom throughout all the lands; the nomadic horsemen were noted for their use of the bow as a weapon.

The connection of the English, Scotch, and Irish fairies to "ghosts" is well known; these ghostly riders were said to have homes in mounds of earth which concealed them, and also in

**112**

# Medusa and Friends

hills and mountains (perhaps suggested by the ancient custom of mound burial of important prehistoric leaders). But one attribute does not preclude another, and the Huns in particular were given lurid and grotesque physical descriptions by the church fathers and authors of the fifth century. The Huns ruled the Ostrogoths for a time, and almost pushed the borders of their empire westward to the Atlantic coast until defeated in battle in France. And the Visigoths before their migrations would also have been beneath the sway of the Huns. The Germanic legends make a connection from the Huns to the Gothic peoples and whatever northern Germanic peoples they may have ruled for a time. The Scandinavians knew of the exploits of the Huns, which might indicate some sort of link to England through the much later Danelaw territory, or through earlier Germanic entries to that land. (The "truth" of legend is irrelevant, in this argument). In any event, the *possible* connection of the British "fairies" to ancient Romans (and sometimes Huns)—as well as to mound-exiting ghosts—deserves at least some consideration due to the size factor, if for no other reason. The Celtic peoples were giants compared to the size of the Romans, and the Scandinavians perhaps even taller than the natives of Gaul or Britain. "Fairies" were always the "little people". It does appear possible that tales of the short and stocky Huns with their bows and arrows and "outlandish" culture and appearance, were more likely to pass from land to land in the antique world through the letters of churchmen, one to another, than through other lanes of communication. The Huns were non-Christian, and were regarded as a sort of "scourge of God" sent as punishment for the sins of society, and there were stories passed that they were the offspring of demons and witches—considered in that light, they must have been thought very dangerous; no goblin or fairy in a tale could be more so.

# ◆ 10 ◀

# A WONDROUS WEIGHT

The legendary Greek musician Orpheus used to cause stones to lift themselves to make walls, and the ancient race of Cyclopes created structures of stones too large to have been moved by mere humans—or so the stories go. Such tales are not confined to the ancient world. Today some people believe in the building skills of "ancient astronauts", mystic crystal "power", ancient telekinesis (moving objects by mental thought-waves), the power of incantations, and lost technology of a "superior" civilization of super-scientists.

We have some difficulty with the idea of lost "super-science", as in general the evidence of change from ancient to modern times seems to support a progressive change from simpler to more sophisticated cultures. It is true that we have lost some knowledge of ancient technologies. As ways of doing things change, some old ways (complex in themselves), may give way to new methods—so that it is not always so easy to repeat a process no longer within our current technological habits. A good example might be the ancient way of preventing the rusting of metal clamps or ties in stone structures found near water. Herodotus stated that in ancient Babylon, bridge builders joined stones with iron and lead (*The Persian Wars*, Modern Library, New York, 1951, p. 100). The ancients seem to have dipped iron into melted lead in order to rust-proof the metal for certain purposes. When in the twentieth century it was decided to repair the ruined Parthenon in Athens, the metal clamps connecting stones were not rust-proofed, and as rust built up the stones cracked due to the thickening of the metal supports. The Athenian engineers, like the Babylonians, had rust-proofed the metal, but modern builders—no longer in the direct ancient tradition—had left out this simple but important step in their repairs. Neither the Babylonians nor the Athenians had been "super scientists", but the knowledge of all necessary steps in their ways of building had been lost through centuries of lack of use.

Some "strange" phenomena (other than the "levitation" of ancient weights), seem to be simply good stories that are told again and again, perhaps with different names and in different settings, and remain alive simply because they *are* good stories. Such seem to be the stories of warning dreams that cause the protagonist to avoid entering an elevator that is destined to fall (described in Melvin Harris' book, *Investigating the Unexplained*, Prometheus Books, Buffalo, 1986, Chapters 12 and 13).

There are some stories that, though they may be repeated time and time again, are yet based (however distantly), on something real. Often one or more elements of a fanciful nature may be added; of this type the Great Stone may be an example.

Andrew Tomas in his book of curiosities *We Are Not the First*, describes a cut stone so large that it would require "forty thousand men" to move it (Bantam Books, New York, 1973 paperback, p. 99). Mr. Tomas does show some restraint. At least he does not claim that it *was* moved. Many writers that have produced books on such subjects as "Atlantis" and "ancient astronauts" have mentioned this stone in contexts that imply or even state that it was hauled around for miles in the ancient past. The great stone supporting imaginative theories is a fact, and yet a fact which has been used out of context. Descriptions of it are met fairly frequently when "strange mysteries" of the past are considered. It has become a "wonder".

The stone does exist. It would measure approximately 72 feet by 16 feet by 16 feet, and weighs about 240,000 pounds. This monster lies in what the Romans used to call Coele Syria (hollow Syria), though within Lebanon's borders in the present day. The site is near the ancient city of Baalbek—the city known also to the ancients as Syrian "City of the Sun" (Syrian Heliopolis, as opposed to the Egyptian Heliopolis), according to some scholars. Called the "Stone of the Pregnant Woman" in arabic, this thing does impress

# A Wondrous Weight

one with its size (a good description, including beautiful illustrations, is found in Friedrich Ragette's *Baalbek*, Chatto & Windus, London, 1980, p. 114; also available in an edition from Noyes Press, Park Ridge, New Jersey, 1980).

Does this mean that the ancients had a capacity to move great weights that we cannot move? The mere reality of this cut stone seems to show that we have indeed lost some peculiar ability once known to builders. But wait.

Suppose that this great stone has *never been moved at all*. Friedrich Ragette, in his *Baalbek*, p. 114, describes this stone as still attached to its base. Perhaps the stone was to be cut later into smaller parts. Perhaps those who cut it had finally cut something too large for their own capacities of transport. But whatever the reason it was not moved; that fact robs it of having been an "impossible" feat. It is not a good example for the believers of the "lost super-science". Still impressive to view, it cannot be regarded as a miracle, and lies where it was (partially) cut.

Sometimes writers state that since no evidence has been found of machines in ancient Egypt, stones must have been lifted in a mysterious or miraculous way. The building of the pyramids has certainly caused some peculiar theories to appear ever since they were constructed, and these "odd" views are still with us. It may be (and, in fact, is very probable), that stones were hauled up ramps and into place by gangs of men building the pyramids. However, it is also true that from very early times the Egyptians had knowledge of a simple counter-weight lifting machine, though in miniature: the scales. Scales evidently were found in their markets or for purposes of business, for we find them pictured in tomb paintings in the theme of "weighing of the heart" against the feather of truth ("Ma'at"). It is also true that, whether lifting machines were or were not used, if they were used they would not have survived. In a country that had to import most of its wood, any construction machines no longer used in building would have long since been cut down for other use—such as furniture or shipbuilding.

There may be an alternate to our concept of the ancient movement of heavy weights by means of rollers. Of course, rollers can be used, as shown by modern attempts to replicate what is taken to be ancient method. But it may be that the use of wooden members pointing ahead (somewhat in the manner of modern railroad tracks), instead of side-wise as rollers, would sometimes be as efficacious as the use of rollers. Such tracks could well allow a weight to be placed upon a sledge and hauled forward; and if oil or grease were applied to the "tracks", the sledge should move with greater facility. One thinks of the slip-ways used to slide ships into the water. In this regard, a study of the illustrations on Page 115 of Ragette's *Baalbek* seems to show two of these elements: in a Mesopotamian style depiction, a weight being moved along "tracks" that point ahead (and some which might act as "rollers"), being pulled by teams of men hauling ropes. The "tracks" are broken—that is, there are spaces between the presumably trimmed logs making the "tracks" and "rollers". In another depiction we see the way that the ancient Egyptians moved great weights. In a depiction of Egyptian style, a weighty statue is being moved on a sledge while a man pours some substance ahead of the sledge. In both depictions, Egyptian and Mesopotamian style art works, the weights being moved rest on sledges. In a curious parallel from American colonial times, according to Alastair Cooke's TV program "America" of a few years ago, colonial farmers moved weights such as stumps and stones from their fields by means of sleds; the sleds worked much better than wheeled vehicles, which tended to become stuck in the earth.

The use of a sledge when moving weights was also employed by the Romans. A large obelisk of Egypt was taken to Alexandria and transported to Italy by water to within three miles of Rome, according to Ammianus Marcellinus. It was then moved by sledge into Rome and placed in the middle of the Circus (Marcellinus, *The Later Roman Empire*, Penguin Books, New York, 1986 paperback, pp. 122-123).

Ragette's book *Baalbek* describes a unique method used by builders of Roman times to lift large and heavy stones. It seems that holes were carved in the tops of the stones, with inclined sides so that the bottom of the holes would be wider than the upper parts; metal inserts were then placed into the holes (known as "lewis holes"), and pushed apart in such a way that a central metal piece could be placed between. Then this insert provided an anchor for lifting upwards by means of block-and-tackle with ropes (Ragette, pp. 116-117). A question arises whether this method was used in initial construction, or only in repair work (perhaps

# A Wondrous Weight

after earthquakes). The second view is taken by J. G. Landels in *Engineering in the Ancient World*, U. of California, 1978, p. 92.

Ragette's fine book describes the ancient temples at the Baalbek site, and mentions visits of early western travellers and the German Kaiser's archaeological expedition of the early twentieth century. The movement of weights of heavy stones in Ragette is considered to have been done with the use of "sleigh" and rollers (p. 115).

Rupert Furneaux in *Ancient Mysteries* (Ballantine Books, New York, 1978 paperback, p. 135), described an experiment sponsored by the BBC in 1954, wherein heavy concrete blocks were moved by the use of rollers and sleds. The lively book *The Ancient Engineers* by L. Sprague de Camp (Ballantine Books, New York, 1987 paperback), describes the use of ropes and sleds in ancient Egypt (pp. 31-35). An interesting idea found in de Camp's study is that milk might be the lubricant used beneath the sled carrying the weight (*The Ancient Engineers*, p. 31).

The use of hard surfaces (supporting the movement of heavy objects from beneath), is seen in the famous case of the construction of the pyramids of Egypt. Pyramid construction may be the subject most discussed by those who hold bizarre theories of "supernatural" methods of construction in ancient societies. But Christine Hobson has described the practical side of the transporting of the weighty stones. In her survey *The World of the Pharaohs* (Thames and Hudson, New York, 1987), she notes that solid causeways were constructed from the bank of the Nile to the site of the pyramid-to-be; after the causeways were smoothed on top, they could support the sledges carrying the heavy stones, pulled by ropes to the building site—with some lubricant being poured upon the causeway in advance of the sledge (pp. 62-63). Large stones cut elsewhere could be shipped by boat to the beginning of the causeway, and there unloaded for the use intended. In Hobson's "causeways", we see the idea from long ago of the use of solid supports across which to move weights.

If large stones could be floated in the air by mumbled incantations or "mind power", then clearly supporting causeways would never be needed. The same is true of transportation by flying saucer.

While the giant stone in modern Lebanon (anciently part of the Roman province of Syria), was never moved, other massive stones were moved. Some of these are found in the wall of Baalbek. Those who wish to make a mystery of the ancient world's ability to apply various types of "mechanical advantage" to weight movement by the use of levers, sledges, or other devices, should use better examples.

Very great stones were used in walls and over doorways in the bronze age cities of Greece such as Tiryns and Mycenae. And, in the time of Josephus, when the Romans beseiged Jerusalem, enormous stones were in place at some points in the defensive walls of that city—those were not good places to attack, for Roman battering rams would not make much of an impression there.

The cutting, hauling, and lifting into place of such great stones was a marvellous thing. Such work was also very difficult. That very difficulty may have been the cause of the fatal division of the Hebrew nation that Solomon's heirs allowed to fall into two parts, for the northern peoples resented the call-up of labor gangs for construction purposes.

Writers who wish to show peculiar and "unexplained" things from the past often copy each other's writings. In the case of the "stone of the pregnant woman" we have a case of an unmoved stone that is erroneously said to have been hauled around in the distant past—while we have shown that it has never been moved at all.

The facts about this stone demonstrate that it may be a good idea to look further when a peculiar or unexpected "fact" is found. More data may change one's view, and explain things that seem unusual at first. Another example might be what we can say about the reason that Athens in the late fifth century lost the Peloponnesian War to Sparta.

Are democracies "weaker" than dictatorships? Not necessarily. We remember Aristotle's dictum that giving each man a share in government may strengthen such government. The failure of Athens in the conflict noted was not due to the type of government that existed in Sparta. If we look more deeply into the historical facts of that conflict, we find that the Persian Empire had supported Sparta. Persia was the only super-power in the whole of the Western world. As the scholar Michael Grant stated, the Athenians had "gratuitously" intervened in Persian internal affairs to aid rebels against the Great King's rule, and that was the chief reason they lost to Sparta (cf. *The Rise of the Greeks*, Charles

# A Wondrous Weight

Scribner's Sons, New York, 1988, p. 282). The evidence for Persian support is overwhelming (Thucydides, *The Peloponnesian War*, Modern Library, New York, 1951, pp. 121, 463, 467, 485, and 515 and other references; Xenophon, *A History of My Times*, Penguin Books, New York, 1983 paperback, pp. 54, 56-57, 99, and 110—this book is by a pro-Spartan person, and is also known as the *Hellenica*). Xenophon's pro-Spartan opinions are so strong that his evidence is particularly impressive. The great English scholar J. B. Bury had the same opinion (e.g. *A History of Greece*, Modern Library, New York, no date given, p. 471). One could pile up many more citations and references to show Persia's intervention. The point is that scholars that argue about "forms of government" are arguing at a remove from the real causes of the defeat of Athens; they see the result, but not the reasons for the result.

Athens was, in fact, tremendously strong. She suffered a terrible plague, the loss of a whole army and navy in Sicily, and the Persian rebuilding of her Spartan enemy's fleet—and still, she almost won. Persia was too wealthy, and Persian gold tipped the balance in Sparta's favor. Rome had not yet risen to be a world power; in the fifth century B.C., Sicily seemed more important than Italy to the Greeks. Alexander the Great would intervene before the later coming of the Romans, and Persia had no equal in strength.

One would not wish to minimize the achievements of the builders of the ancient world, who did produce some most impressive feats of construction. This should be taken as proof of human effort, skill, and imagination, and not as some sort of miracle. The "miraculous" view robs the builders of credit for their own very real ability.

The use of sledges is a natural way to move very heavy objects, once one thinks of it. When Thor Heyerdahl's expedition to Easter Island desired the untutored natives to move a great stone statue from the place it was carved, the natives thought of the idea of a sledge at once, cut a tree with a "V" branching, and used it underneath the statue. With ropes attached to the improvised sledge, the statue was moved without too great a degree of difficulty (see Ronald Story's *The Space-Gods Revealed: A Close Look at the Theories of Erich von Daniken*, Harper & Row, New York, 1976, pp. 50-51; also p. 64 for probable use in Egypt of sledges). The natives, watched by Heyerdahl and the other members of his

**121**

expedition, were able to haul the great stone statues quite a distance, and were capable of setting them up by gradually levering them upward with the help of piles of stones.

Since the Egyptian work of art shows how the ancient Egyptians did in fact move weights, it certainly seems an out-of-place effort for authors to invoke incantations, mind power, or flying saucers as a means of such transportation. (Those who wish to view the ancient Egyptian art work that shows a weight being moved should see F. Ragette's *Baalbek,* p. 115 of either the English or American edition—the page numbers seem to be the same in both editions; see book descriptions as listed earlier in this chapter.)

# ▶ 11 ◀
# WEREDOG

Men have long feared the "werewolf"—and rightly so. For the creature was thought to be a man turned into a wolf, and we all know that man is a dangerous animal. The belief that people could change their shape is an ancient belief, and may have its origin as far back as the stone age; the shaman figure (comparable to the "medicine man" of the American Indian peoples), is very ancient.

There is a reference in Herodotus (*Persian Wars*, Modern Library edition, p. 333), in his Book IV, to a people who turned "into a wolf" once a year: the Neurians. These were said to be neighbors of the Scythians, who vouched for the tale. Presumably ancient shamans were noted for trances and "out of body" experiences, the achievement of which might put them in touch with the "spirit world"; sometimes this might be achieved with the aid of an animal "spirit" helper. The scholar Michael Grant, in *The Rise of the Greeks*, (Charles Scribner's Sons, New York, 1988, pp. 229, 304, 308), traced the arrival in Greece of such beliefs that travelled from the land of the Scythians, through Thrace, and into Greece—with the result of the introduction of new types of miracle-mongering. Scythians lived to the north-east of the Greeks, and Thrace was intermediate between those nomads and them; and the colonies that the Greeks had planted on the north coast of the Black Sea would encounter the Scythians more directly (Grant, p. 308).

The Greeks of the south had a wolf-god Apollo "Lykios" (J.

**123**

# Beasts and Battles

B. Bury, *A History of Greece*, Modern Library, p. 842 note to p. 128), and the wolf helped found Rome, in a sense. But the "werewolf" was somewhat different. He is ancient as well, as noted in Charlotte F. Otten, editor, *A Lycanthropy Reader: Werewolves in Western Culture*, (Syracuse University Press, Syracuse, 1986 paperback, Chapters 20 and 21); he's in Greece and Rome, in the stories of Ovid and Petronius.

The origin of the werewolf idea may be found in the shamanistic practises alluded to, although such was not the shaman's purpose. A "werewolf" shaman would definitely be a shaman "gone bad". The memory of the werewolf was kept fresh in England and France (he was called "loup-garou" in the French usage)—possibly by memory of the Vikings and their raids. Some Vikings apparently worked themselves into a "wolfish" frame of mind for battle, and were known as "wolf-coats" (Otten, pp. 148-150). The wearing of skins of wolves for what we would call "war magic", and the name of "wolf-coat" could certainly suggest a blood-thirsty beast and lead directly to a werewolf concept. The saga heroes Sigmund and Sinfjotli turned into wolves when they put on wolf skins that they could not remove except after a certain number of days (Otten, pp. 151-152). Merely wearing a belt made of wolf skin might cause one to become a werewolf (Otten, pp. 149-150).

There is a theme in the literature of the werewolf that has to do with the "magical" power of human clothing. This theme is seen in the twelfth century tale of Marie de France in which the hero has to have access to his clothing in order to regain his human shape (Otten, Chapter 23, and e.g. p. 257). The werewolf is said to be called by the name of "Garwal" in Normandy, and named "Bisclaveret" in Brittany (Otten, p. 256). In some of these early tales the werewolf is the hero—really a good fellow who is schemed against by others, often with illicit love as the motive of those who either cause his misery, or take advantage of it.

The theme of the use of human clothing as the restorer of humanity emerges even in the twentieth century, and in Burma. Whether a native superstition or one brought to that land from Europe or elsewhere, it seems that the Burmese natives used to believe in the existence of a were *tiger*. This belief was current in the first half of the 1900's, if the jungle hunter Jack Girsham is to be believed (see *Burma Jack*, by Jack Girsham and Lowell

# Weredog

Thomas, W. W. Norton, New York, 1971, pp. 102 and 104-108). The Burmese were-tiger would become "human" again if his wife brought his clothes and dropped them near him.

The idea of the shaman and his animal helper may run further back in time than we might expect, perhaps all the way to the Old Stone Age. There are portrayals of what seem to be men wearing animal masks (and perhaps skins). The so-called "Sorceror" figure from the French "Three Brothers" cave site is an example. The "spirit helper" of the shaman might be almost any sort of animal.

There is a scene of a man (falling or in a trance), bird on a stock or wand, and a wounded bison; this scene is again from a French cave, the famous Lascaux. In the September, 1988 issue of the journal *Antiquity*, there is a short piece about this scene by Davenport and Jochim ("The Scene in the Shaft at Lascaux", pp. 558-562). In that piece, the observation is made that the male figure may be that of a shaman turning himself into a bird (or already "turned"), as indicated by his four fingers; birds have four toes, and the figure on the wand or stick represents a bird spirit "helper". We have here not a werewolf, but rather a were-Grouse. The argument is persuasive. If we accept this argument for the antiquity of shamanism (and it seems that we can), then it becomes even more surprising that an animal "helper" idea could leap into life again in the concepts of witchcraft and the witch's "familiar". The extreme duration through time of this idea (evidently some 30,000 years), is a thing of amazement in itself.

The werewolves seemed to strike in France in the 18th century. From 1764 to 1767 there took place a very odd series of "man-eater" attacks by "wolves"—some thought by werewolves. Victims were numerous: somewhat less or somewhat more than 100 persons. When one of the beasts was killed, the great French naturalist Buffon pronounced that the culprit was a big wolf.

The attacks took place in the south of France, in rough country, and in an area inhabited by large numbers of wolves. Nevertheless, the peoples of this area were not afraid to send very young children out on "guard duty" to take care of cattle and sheep. There was no fear of non-rabid wolves.

Most of the victims were very young children. Some children had fought and beaten off the attacker, and had reported attack by a large wolf. This beast, the so-called "Beast of Gévaudan",

# Beasts and Battles

seems to fly in the face of the American claims about the "peaceful" and "non-dangerous" nature of wolves (see, for example, L. David Mech's *The Wolf*, Natural History Press, Garden City, 1970, pp. 289-294). But we may yet save the reputation of the wolf, even in the case of the "Beast".

There is an excellent examination of the case of the "Beast" in an article in the April, 1971 issue of *Natural History* magazine. In his article, "The Beast of Gévaudan", C. H. D. Clarke shows that the real culprit (or culprits, since there seem to be more than one "beast" in the case), might in all probability have been a hybrid mix of dog and wolf. Clarke points out that: 1) there were at least two "Beasts"; 2) they were unusually large for wolves; 3) they had markings not usual for wolves (one had a white throat color, and the other had a "reddish" coat as remarked by the naturalist Buffon when he examined the remains); 4) they were not rabid; and 5) they did stalk people. People bitten in the face did not die, if they were able to escape their attackers; and the wolves ate the bodies of those they killed. These facts indicate that the wolves were not rabid. Clarke makes a good case for the animals in question being a dog-wolf cross, rare and almost never known in nature in the wild; yet the man-eating creatures called "Beast" engaged in the habit of attacking, killing, and eating people—an activity also almost never known in nature. The likelihood of these animals being trained dogs seems low, for both apparently had mates in the wild, one with pups. The two evident culprits were both killed in the wild, and so were their mates.

It may well be that feral dogs are more dangerous to man than wolves. In this connection, one wonders if some tales of attacks in France from earlier centuries may be seen to be possible *dog attacks*. The evidence that led authorities in the old days (16th and 17th centuries) to point to "werewolf" attackers seem to also, in at least one direction, point to dogs. This clue is the evidence of the wolf "without a tail" (cf. Otten, *A Lycanthropy Reader*, pp. 79, 86, 87). Clearly, many more dogs than wolves would have their tails cropped. To be attacked by a dog is not very romantic, and a "wolf" attack makes a better story for one to tell his neighbors. Dogs are less in awe of people than are wolves. Clarke's article on the case of the "Beast" implicates them as well as wolves—and perhaps more so.

Italy in the 14th century had a certain population of wolves

# Weredog

(some of which still exist today). Barbara Tuchman has a note on travel conditions in 1343 in Calabria and Apulia, showing that people had no need of arms, but only of clubs to beat off dogs (*A Distant Mirror: The Calamitous 14th Century*, Ballantine Books, 1978 paperback, New York, p. 398). (To be fair, she also wrote that wolves attacked people in Paris in famine conditions—cf. p. 592; but could these have been packs of dogs?). Under normal conditions, then, one might have to beat off dogs, but not wolves.

There are tales out of Russia that sometimes wolves had been known to chase sleighs in the winter. Some say these tales are myths, but it would be perfectly natural for a wolf to do this sort of thing, for he would be *chasing the horse or horses*, his natural prey.

Because non-rabid wolves are more or less harmless, it may not be a particularly good idea to re-introduce them into areas from which they were removed in the past. There is too much danger of their being shot up and destroyed yet once again, as is still being done in Alaska.

Werewolves, which do not exist, would have been very dangerous because of their human part, as we said at the beginning of this chapter. But just out of sight and lurking in the shadows of this theme is our old friend the dog. Most dogs are nice. They are loyal, friendly, and good companions. But, gone to the wild, they are dangerous. They are dangerous singly, as in the case of the Pit Bull of recent years, bred to attack without remorse or second thoughts. As reported in the January 30, 1989 *Time* magazine, the Health Commissioner of New York City desires to have such dogs muzzled, insured, tatooed, and photographed for city records before they appear in public (see p. 31). Instead of being harsh, such measures might well be prudent in an era when dogs are being deliberately bred for cruel and vicious traits.

Alexander the Great met some tough-minded dogs in India. They were used in hunts for lions, and seemingly four were a match for one lion. To demonstrate their single-mindedness in the hunt, four were put upon a lion, and an Indian pulled on the leg of one dog. When the dog would not let go his grip on the lion, the Indian cut off his leg. When he still would not be moved from his prey, the Indian cut him in other places, and kept on slashing at him until he died; but he died with his teeth still in the lion (see *The History of Alexander*, by Quintus Curtius Rufus, Penguin

# Beasts and Battles

Books, New York, 1984 paperback, p. 214). This may show great inhumanity, but it also shows that dogs can be dangerous. Feral dogs that run in packs are doubly dangerous. The wild dogs of both Africa and India can terrify animals larger and seemingly more dangerous than they; even lions and tigers are not safe from them. Domestic dogs that have "gone wild" and run in packs can also be dangerous, and it is probable that they are considerably more dangerous than wolves. Wolves, unless they have rabies, have a certain awe of people, and a great degree of caution concerning them (entertainment media to the contrary notwithstanding).

Animals that appear more cunning or resourceful than other animals are looked on as "more than" animal. Just as the Beast of Gévaudan was thought of by some as a werewolf, a creature more than wolf, so the natives of India seemed to react to the rampages of tigers and leopards. Some few of these animals became man-eaters due to old age or wounds, and were terribly successful at that career, being able to do away with hundreds of people. This sort of seemingly invincible rampage in the time of Jim Corbett, the great British hunter of man-eaters, caused the natives to believe that the tiger or leopard was a "spirit" creature that could not be killed—until Corbett ended these problems (the accounts were detailed in his *Man-Eaters of Kumaon* (New York: Oxford University Press, 1946), and other books.

The dog again emerges as villain in the recent case in Australia, made into the motion picture *A Cry in the Dark*, starring Meryl Streep. The wild dog of Australia called the "dingo" had killed and carried off an unfortunate woman's young child while it was unattended. And periodically in England, mysterious "beasts" kill livestock at night; these are almost certainly dogs that have "gone bad".

Man's ancient helper in the hunt can turn from ally to enemy. The various creatures which could long ago function as the shaman's "spirit helper" can—become an enemy and "outlaw" for whatever reasons—be transformed into instruments of destruction and unreasoning fear to many people. They may fill our dreams with terror, whether the dangers are real or only products of superstition.

The "werewolf" Beast of Gévaudan has turned into a less terrible figure: a "weredog", if you will. A figure to be respected, but not one with the mythos of the wolf attached. We can remove

THE FIRST "WEREWOLF"? Egyptian priest wearing the mask of Anubis, the jackal god of the Underworld. If Arelene Wolinski is correct, the two elements dangling down the figure's chest from the jackal's head indicate that the figure is a masked priest, and not a god. (Drawing by the author from illustration in Wolinski's article "Egyptian Masks: The Priest and His Role", p. 22 of the magazine *Archaeology*, Vol. 40, No. 1, Jan./Feb. 1987). This figure in processions and ceremonies would be both eye-catching and easily liable to misunderstanding by Greeks and Romans in pre-Christian Egypt.

The cult of Anubis was introudced to Rome as one of Hermes-Anubis or Mercury-Anubis, and figures were therefore seen in Roman tunics parading Rome's streets in the Mask here shown; Roman men of letters and an early Christian church father commented on the sight. Thus a seeming "wolf-man" must have been seen in Rome by the Germanic soldiers defending the Empire; (cf. Wolinski, esp. pp. 28 and 29).

the silent shadows of fear from that account, at least, thanks to Clarke's convincing magazine article which examined intelligently the French evidence. Due to his efforts, we perceive that the tale of that "Beast" is very likely the tale of a creature that was in large part a dog (or part dog and part wolf, as Clarke contended in his *Natural History* magazine article cited above).

The very idea of the "werewolf" may be a sort of dog's fault, in a way. If recent contentions are correct, the ancient Egyptian priests of the gods wore masks constructed of a sort of papier-maché, and may have walked in processions and taken part in ceremonies wearing them (see Arelene Wolinski's "Egyptian Masks: The Priest and His Role" in the magazine *Archaeology*, Vol. 40, No. 1, Jan./Feb. 1987, pp. 22-29). The god Anubis (the jackal-faced god), wore a mask with an appearance strikingly similar to that of a wolf; and the Romans even had statues of an Anubis-Mercury, or Hermes-Anubis, showing a man with the jackal head—scorned by the Romans as a dog's head, (Wolinski shows a photograph of one such statue on p. 29, *op. cit.*). The Greeks traded with Egypt from very early days, and later were hired as mercenary soldiers; even later they established the kingdom of Ptolemy there. Still later the Romans came and occupied Egypt, and until Christian times, all of those would have been able to observe the Anubis-priest in his mask. This gives us a possible origin to the "werewolf" belief that is different from Scythian shaman beliefs as filtered through Thrace into Greece in ancient times, and also different from Viking "ber-serks" working themselves into a rage while pretending to be animals.

Medieval Europeans who lived a wild outlaw life in the forest, robbing and killing their victims, might well be called wolves in a sort of poetic comparison.

# ◆ 12 ◆

# TIME MACHINE GODS?

The concept of a "time machine" is an interesting one. In movies or science fiction stories, the hero enters a contraption, sets a switch, and disappears from the present time into the past or future. But most, if not all, of these scenarios overlook one very important fact: the *"time machine" would have to be a space ship as well*, very likely.

Since our earth moves through space, circling around the sun (while the sun moves also, carrying the planets with it on its cruise through space), we are part of a vast formation that travels through space all the time. The natural result of this movement is that the earth will have been in a different place in the past from where it is now; and, in the future, it will yet again be in a different place. It moves all the while. This means that we will have to probably have a capability in our "time machine" to set our course for a certain place as well as a certain time, and run the risk of arriving in outer space somewhere if we miss our target place and time. Therefore, our time machine must carry its own oxygen-nitrogen atmosphere just in case we arrive out in space. We will need a computer to set our course, since travelling through time as well as space (or "space-time", as it were), will be too complicated for anyone to do the mathematics of course setting in their head. Only an age that can produce an air-tight and inhabitable environment (a space ship, in other words), can produce a time machine that is viable. We must remember Copernicus and Galileo when we build our time-travel device, or run the risk of stranding ourselves in outer space without knowing "where" we are, resulting in our own destruction. A simple point, but one overlooked by our writers of more imaginative fiction.

Secondary problems will arise in the building of our machine: it will have to be so constructed as to protect the occupant(s) from the trip itself: if we go "to the past", we must not regress to the status of an embryo and die; and if we go "to the future", we must not wither away and perish from old age! So the environment within the machine must be able to be independent of the exterior temporal fluctuations. The "interior time" must remain in the "present" and separate from the "exterior time" which changes. If these problems are not solved, it will do us no good to produce a device that travels through time, for no one will be able to make use of it.

Our twentieth century technology obviously does not yet possess the abilities requisite to the construction of a time machine. But that does not mean that we (or someone else), might not be capable of building such a thing in the future. Have we been visited by such means in our time or in the past? Given the huge size of the universe that our astronomers have discovered, the visit by a time machine from the future ages of our own earth seems far more likely than a visit from "space travellers" from some other planet. The earth itself is but a speck—a distant grain of dust in a vast and tremendously spacious universe; we should logically be hard to locate or visit. We are like a grain of sand lost in the myriad sands of a beach that stretches to the distance upon every side of us.

Is time travel even conceivably possible? Since the modern view is that neither time nor space is "absolute" in the old Newtonian sense, we cannot be sure of the answer. From time to time physicists speculate on the possible use of Black Holes for time travel, and in the January 16, 1989 issue of *Time* magazine there is an article on the use of the so-called "wormholes" in time travel (p. 55). The article seems to conclude that such travel is unlikely, since the wormholes are so minute.

Some have theorized that if one could somehow surpass the limit of the speed of light, then one might enter a zone of temporal reversing. The speed of light is an absolute limit, as well as being the constant yardstick for Einstein's Special Theory of Relativity. But Einstein himself wrote that it is not a limit in his

# Time Machine Gods?

General Theory. Insofar as any practical use could be made of any of these concepts, that remains another matter. Presumably, if one could reach the speed of light, one would be caught in an unending static state and be forever unable to move—time would "stop" altogether, and one might well "become" light (be translated from a state of matter into a state of energy completely), insofar as an outside observer is concerned. None of these events would seem especially helpful.

Of course, as one speeds up relative to the outside world, the faster one travels, the slower one's "interior" time in relation to the time that passes in the "exterior" world. In that limited sense, "time travel" is possible—but not very much time is gained unless one approaches the speed of light, which is more difficult and not now practicable in the current state of our scientific knowledge.

Many of our science fiction writers have developed stories based on concepts such as the variations in time and in matter caused by speed—though they have neglected the idea of space travel being directly related to time travel, again remembering Galileo and Copernicus.

And the fact that space may be "curved" in some areas need not trouble us unduly; we all understand clearly that the course set across an ocean may be a curve instead of a straight line. Indeed, any travel across the surface of a solid sphere must be a curved path by definition. In fact, the idea that gravity may "bend" space may be a clue to the future ability to *seem* to travel "faster than light" by taking advantage of spatial convolutions in order to "jump" from one place in space to another without going "the long way" between places; such concepts are fairly standard in science fiction writing. When a spaceship in such a story makes such a "jump", it is usually said by the author to be entering "hyperspace". But, even though these ideas are not new, they do us no real good in considering the theory of time travel as a practical thing to be achieved in our time.

Is there any evidence that other and future ages have achieved time travel? Has our earth been visited by such means in the past?

In Homer's *Iliad*, Hephaistos, the smith of the gods, seems to have robot helpers and automated machinery to help him (Book 18, Lines 373-377, 417-420, and 468-473). If not, what are we to make

# Beasts and Battles

of self-propelled wheeled tripods, golden robots that look like young women and have the power of movement to assist their master, and bellows for forging metal that can "follow orders"? The last sounds like machinery that runs on a "program" of some sort.

Again, what are we to make of the ancient automaton that guards the island of Crete. This entity appears in the story of Jason and the Golden Fleece: the writings of one Apollonius of Rhodes, called the *Argonautica* (see, for instance, *The Voyage of Argo*, E. V. Riew translation, Penguin Classics, 1959 paperback, p. 191). The giant named "Talos" ran around Crete three times a day and prevented strangers from landing on the shores. He was destroyed by Jason's lover Medea, through the use of extra-sensory perception (early ESP). What's more, this metallic monster was descended from a whole race of like creatures (mentioned on the same page).

Were the gods of the ancient Greeks "ancient astronauts" from other worlds—spacemen superior to the mere "earthlings" of our world? It would seem not: the gods and goddesses were able to have children by mortal men and women, and we know that divergent species cannot breed successfully. Taking the ancient tales at face value, we perceive that this ability to breed points to earthly similarity. And we have already noted the not very likely possibility of being found by others from among the stars, using the argument of the size of the universe. Theseus was the son of Poseidon, god of the Sea, and a mortal woman, and Hercules was the son of Zeus and a mortal woman. Aneas, who founded Rome in Virgil's poem, was the son of the Roman goddess Venus (Greek Aphrodite).

Were the Greek gods "time travellers" from our own future? Future people emerging from a time machine to lord it over the unsophisticated peoples of a bygone age? Many of the abilities of these deities can be matched by the technology of the late twentieth century. People can fly—not only in airplanes, but with individual back-pack jets. We can make "thunder" with sticks and kill at a distance (using rifles or handguns). We can put a cloak of "darkness" around ourselves or others (by the use of a "smoke screen"). We can move very rapidly over great distances. Are our descendants of the future the "gods" of ancient Greece?

The name of the father of Zeus, Chronos, sounds very much like a name for time itself (compare our word "chronology"). The gods and goddesses, when cut, did not bleed blood. They bled "ichor". And in our time there has been developed a clear liquid in which a mouse can breathe and remain alive, though submerged in it. And genetics is our most rapidly advancing field of science today. Did we create automatons with superior abilities for some purpose, which then somehow escaped into the past? The Greek gods were called "immortal", but they may have simply been extremely long-lived. Again, we are making some progress in extending life, though we have far to go. Some in the past believed that at least one divine or semi-divine being had died: Pan, the entity that created fear when he wished, and played upon musical pipes in the forests of a time long past.

We only need one time-traveller to begin the race of "gods". Zeus produced Athena "from his head"—perhaps in a test-tube? Dionysus was born from a thigh: was he a clone, created from cells of an extant "deity"? Was Zeus an archaeologist/historian sent to the past to gather data, that then deceived Chronos ("Time"?), his "father", by placing a stone in the time machine that brought him to the past?

Does all this point to the Greek gods as time-travellers?

Not necessarily.

In a more orthodox perspective of history, we remember the clever mechanical devices of the intellectual artisans of Ptolemaic Alexandria. Hero (Greek Heron) and those who came before and after him provided a veritable plethora of full-sized and miniature device plans for mechanical "wonders", some of which were built. Though these may have been fabricated for religious use (statues that moved, coin-operated holy waters dispensers, etc.); and may have been made for entertainment (horse that drank water and never "lost his head" as a sword was passed completely through his neck); they would have been an obvious stimulus to the imaginations of those who copied and wrote commentaries upon the works of the authors of the past. (For some of these devices see Landels, J. G., *Engineering in the Ancient World*, U. of California Press, 1978, esp. pp. 199-208; the horse is pictured in *Dunninger's Complete Encyclopedia of Magic*, Spring Books, New York, no date, pp. 66-67).

The lighting of temple fires secretly by seemingly "miraculous" means, or the putting a light inside a statue to make its eyes shine, might even impress a modern person not used to these

## Beasts and Battles

sorts of tricks. Michael Grant lists some of these devices in his *From Alexander to Cleopatra*, Charles Scribner's Sons, New York, 1982, p. 230. Such tricks would impress and even frighten people who viewed them; in our age they are used in the illusions of stage magicians, and not in religious context. The Greeks of the city of Alexandria in Egypt under the rule of the Ptolemies were very clever people. As shown in many ancient writings, the Greeks and Romans had a habit of "tempering" their wine. This simply meant the addition of water to dilute the strength of the wine, so that it could be drunk throughout a social evening for a longer time. They looked upon the drinking of untempered wine as somewhat uncouth and barbaric. Perhaps because of these habits, the Alexandrians devised pitchers that would pour wine or water, or wine "tempered" with water (Grant, p. 230; also mentioned in L. Sprague de Camp's *The Fringe of the Unknown*, Prometheus Books, 1983 paperback, Chapter 6 and especially p. 47).

The tricks of being able to cause a "spontaneous" fire on an altar must have been useful from time to time for the priests of particular locales, who might expect some reward or donation to the deity of the place if the "miracle" occurred while a notable person was nearby; this "good omen" was taken seriously by some of the ancients. Suetonius relates one such event that was evidently taken to be evidence of divine favor for Tiberius (Suetonius, *The Twelve Caesars*, Penguin Books, 1987 paperback; "Tiberius" 14, p. 122). The ancient classical world had its share of omens, miracles, signs, and portents.

Would the intellectuals of Alexandria have dared to insert additional passages in such valued works as the *Iliad?* Homer's *Iliad*, originating from probably the eighth century B.C., was perhaps the most valued and widely known work in the ancient Greek pagan world. It lasted for more than one thousand years as the chief cultural treasure of the Hellenistic peoples, and was still known in the later Christian era, as it is today. It was said that Alexander the Great carried a copy with him on campaign, which had been edited especially for him by his old tutor, Aristotle.

Nevertheless, it may be that the copyists and commentators of Alexandria (or even earlier), might have inserted some few lines of their own in the great classic.

Some believe that the Athenians had added a description of fifty Athenian ships to the list of those that sailed against Troy

# Time Machine Gods?

(known as the "Catalogue of the Ships" in the *Iliad*, Book 2, Lines 546-556; on this see Pausanias, *Guide to Greece*, Vol. 1, p. 10, note 7; Penguin Books, New York, 1985 paperback). This belief about tampering with the *Iliad* is also mentioned in Michael Grant's *Roman Myths*, Dorset Press, no town listed, 1984, p. 68.

If the lines about the ships were added, it is equally possible that later additions might also have taken place: some few lines might have been written into the description of the meeting of Achilles' mother Thetis with the smith Hephaistos, in order to secure new armor for her son.

The *Voyage of Argo* by Apollonius was from a far later date in its composition, although dealing with a purportedly earlier event (since Hercules is in the story of Jason and the Golden Fleece, and he is one or two generations older than Helen of Troy herself—this being only "legendary" order of events, of course). Apollonius' work would be in no way so sacrosanct as the *Iliad* of Homer, and there might be little compunction about adding material to the tale of Jason's wanderings and adventures, in order to "spice up" the story somewhat. Apollonius was resident in Alexandria, but before the time of Hero; still, some early devices may have been known to him, so that he may have used his own imagination to extend somewhat any simpler early devices that he may have seen, in order to present the metal giant Talos of Crete in his *Argonautica.*

All this supposes that scholars producing versions of books for sale would be capable of inserting "wonders" and devices into books that they edited. If, as Michael Grant notes in his *Roman Myths*, p. 68, they might alter literature for patriotic reasons, that does not necessarily mean that they would do so for reasons of entertainment. We here note that possibility, while admitting that the scholars do not say so; and also admitting that these early machines may simply be products of the human talent and imagination of the writers (though Homer seems awfully early to have produced descriptions of female robots that move and do work). Since our knowledge of the ancient world is very piece-meal and limited, it may be that some mechanical constructs were fabricated in that world far earlier than the time that Alexander founded the city of Alexandria in Egypt. But, since that city was the intellectual capitol of the Hellenistic world, and contained the great library,

# Beasts and Battles

we must wonder if copyists in that city had some part in the appearance of the machines in the ancient books mentioned.

There is another theory of time travel. Some believe that there are places on this earth where time "warps" or bends in peculiar ways, which may allow or even force the entry of objects or people into past or future times. Such a place is said to be the "Bermuda Triangle". This theory is not easy to prove. If there are "doorways in time", so to speak, it will be hard to determine if these exist, or if they are simply produced as good stories. We will leave the theme open, subject to future proof—the evidence as offered so far being inconclusive

The sinking of ships in the "Bermuda Triangle" becomes less mysterious when we remember the storms that periodically create dangers of a natural kind. The Spanish treasure ships that have been the object of searches for many years were the victims of such periodic rampages of nature. The number of losses must include the private yachts that may have run afoul of their owners' intoxication and lack of navigational skill, in addition to the normal hazards of the weather. These more understandable factors serve to explain accounts that otherwise might make us pause to wonder at an unknown, but we will readily admit that unknowns do exist.

# ◆ 13 ◆

# DISCOVERING AMERICA

Some mysteries seem to be quite simple on the face of it. When Marco Polo travelled to the court of the Great Khan, ruler of China, he observed various animals that were trained to hunt. Among these were huge lions, with orange, black, and white stripes. We know at once that these "striped lions" had to be tigers, however amazing it seems to us that anyone could train them to the hunt. We know that Marco Polo did not walk into a "fifth dimension" and observe beasts of an irregular and exotic type that are not normally seen on earth. These tigers were taken to the hunt in cages, and there are questions we would like to ask about the whole process—but we would add this case to our short list of "solved" legendary creatures (see Marco Polo's *The Travels*, Penguin Books, New York, 1982, p. 142, for an account of the striped lions).

There are other questions that are not so simple, such as the puzzle of behaviour and inherited characteristics. For example, according to an expert hunter who knew them very well, tigers have no sense of smell. Yet they behave as though they are aware of scent and its meaning to other animals. The tiger stalks its prey in such a way as to avoid giving it the tiger's own scent. Thus, if you are in danger of attack by a man-eater (of which there are very few), then you should be safer walking with your back to the wind, in which case the only directions of attack you need consider would be from the sides (see Jim Corbett's book *The Temple Tiger*, New York: Oxford University Press, 1955, pp. 32, 115, 174). Cats prefer to attack from behind, but how does the tiger "know" which locations he should prefer, insofar as the breeze direction is concerned? The answer we most prefer these days would be that tigers that took account of wind direction had more success in the hunt, and so left more offspring again and again through the ages, until such behaviour became fixed.

Other mysteries, or gaps in our knowledge, seem to be created by the simple fact that we do not have enough data to make any definitive judgement about certain subjects. In the case of the peopling of the New World, we do have good evidence that man first came to North America from what is now Siberia, and that such entry may have taken place some ten to twelve thousand years ago.

But there is not a great deal of evidence, and we could use a lot more. We need to discover many more sites of early occupation, and we need to await thorough and very detailed analyses of such places. We do not have enough evidence to exclude occupation of both continents of the New World from very early times—perhaps tens of thousands of years ago—nor enough to point to such early occupation. The experts in the field still contest dates of as long ago as 40,000 or more years.

This is a case upon which anger should be limited until considerably more evidence is produced and weighed by people competent to do so. The word "impossible" does not yet apply to the idea of very ancient occupation (meaning by "ancient" perhaps some thirty thousand years ago or even older than that). One thing forgotten sometimes is that *the very earliest sites of occupation in the New World may never be located.* The simple reason is that—during certain times of the Ice Ages—the level of oceans dropped markedly: perhaps more than two hundred feet. If in very early times small groups of hunters had crossed from Siberia to Alaska (and note: this does not necessitate a "land bridge", as people can use boats or cross on ice in winter); and if such peoples had drifted south, either in boats or on foot along the coast—then early camp sites along the shore will be located today under two hundred or more feet of water. For the sea level has risen.

We have today accepted that "civilization" began with the use of agriculture in a large way, perhaps some six thousand (or even a little more) years ago. The surplus of food obtained in such use allowed leisure for some, and the fixed location of the houses allowed accumulation and storage of goods as well as food. Such goods, and eventually clay tablet records, would have been far too cumbersome to be carried by wandering hunter-gatherers. And the increased population made possible by the increased food supply, in conjunction with communication with other such locations and early gift-giving or trade routes, made possible the advances which produced what we call "civilization": life in cities, and the things that go with such a life.

The above account is, of course, a very abbreviated and simplified history. We might well note here that people only on the level of hunter-gatherers seem to have a very great amount of leisure. Leisure alone is not enough to produce the "fruits" of civilization.

Storage of grain gave early peoples insurance against the future as well as leisure for some of the members of the early societies. We are aware of yet another food source that also provides such insurance: fish. Fish can be stored in large quantities for future use: it can be sun-dried, smoked, and salted, and the creatures that produce this source were once abundant along the coasts of oceans in many places. Fish could be stock-piled as well as Mesopotamian grain.

This is not to say that the use of stored fish could produce an early pre-agricultural "civilization". But it does point to a *possibility* of early occupation sites on the shores of continents—or island coasts—that cannot be found; for if such sites are ancient enough, they would now be under the ocean at a considerable depth, and so could not be found, barring great advances in undersea archaeology.

It is sometimes said that ancient ships could never cross from Europe to the New World, but it is evident that they could—in our time people have crossed the Atlantic in small boats (even a row-boat); with enough luck, almost any ship or boat could cross. The real question is: Would anyone try? And the answer is: Most would not.

Scholars are agreed that ancient sailors in the time of, say, Greece as late as the classical period, would not like to sail out of sight of land unless compelled; and they would need to be able to be near enough to land to replenish food supplies, and especially water. It was useful to be able to pull one's boat up on shore in the event of a coming storm. The Greeks of Hesiod's time and later also thought it unwise to even sail in the Mediterranean Sea in winter.

The peoples from Europe most likely to visit the New World would have been the Phoenicians, and especially their descendants, the Carthaginians. But the Carthaginians had a very good reason *not* to sail to the New World: profit and loss. They were businessmen with a commercial empire. The trip was just too long for any cargo except gold or silver. Timber could be had in Europe. The peoples of the arctic north of Europe could come to the New World, though they would be more likely to remain in the more northerly areas, in living conditions that they knew well. Later Vikings came and stayed for awhile, but it was not commercially to their interest to stay permanently. A thousand years ago the natives were dangerous—probably provoked by the Vikings themselves. What was commercially not feasible for the Vikings would be even less so for peoples based much further away.

That is not to say that individual men of daring spirit might not have explored the New World even in the time of the early Greeks, Romans, or Carthaginians. If they had, they would have been most likely to come sailing by the so-called "northern route" so that they could travel from land-fall to land-fall: making the island stops on the way. First the Shetlands, then the Faeroes, then Iceland, then Greenland, and Newfoundland. Going from land, to land, to land would be in keeping with the ancient sailing methods. For these reasons, it would be very interesting to have archaeological surveys in some depth of all these "stopping" places, for the sake of curiosity, if nothing else.

For the same reason, it would be of some interest to obtain a thorough survey of the Cape Hatteras area using the most modern methods of undersea archaeology. Would such a place, notorious for storms and danger to seamen, yield any evidence of ancient shipwreck?

There were old Irish tales of the voyage of a monk or church leader named Brendan. These interesting tales claim various "oversea" sites of monasteries, and in one place visited, Brendan and his crew had to dodge hot iron thrown at them by uncivil strangers. The Vikings at their site in L'Anse aux Meadows in Newfoundland had worked with iron; if Brendan's voyage had been put some three or four hundred years later by the sources, one could even predict such a greeting for a churchman from a Viking such as

# Discovering America

Erik the Red (who hated the Christian Church, and held to the old pagan ways). The Vikings left Newfoundland, and the monks of even earlier times, if any, left little or no trace in America.

There were legends of a Welsh Prince named Madoc, said by some to have discovered America in 1170 A.D., though there is no evidence that this tale, used for political reasons by the English in the time of Elizabeth the 1st, had any validity. But the Irish may have reached Iceland before the Vikings (see *Madoc*, by Gwyn A. Williams, New York: Oxford University Press, 1987 paperback, p. 53). Williams details the search for evidence of Madoc in the New World, but his conclusion is: lack of evidence. (There is an interesting reference to a "Fountain of Youth" believed by the Welsh of long ago to be located on the Island of Lundy in England's Bristol Channel. Much earlier, Herodotus gave an account of a people located south of Egypt called the "long-lived" Ethiopians, who attained great age by virtue of using certain waters. Ref. Williams' *Madoc*, p. 52; and Herodotus, Modern Library edition, p. 221.)

Several hundred or more years ago, there was some thought that the American Indians might be the "lost tribes of Israel". But, of course, the "lost" tribes were not lost at all, and had simply preferred to remain in Mesopotamia when freed by the Persians from their Babylonian captivity.

It is not altogether impossible for early ships running south along the east coast of Africa to be driven much further south and come upon Antarctica, and then to travel north up the east coast of South America at an early time. If such a thing happened, it would not be Egyptian sailors who made such a trip. Despite Thor Heyerdahl's heroic trip in a reed boat, the Egyptians were great stay-at-homes. The likely sailors in such a scenario, who might have been driven south along Africa's east coast, would be Arabic—and if driven south along the west coast, Carthaginian or Phoenician. Such trips are not impossible, but would not be regular or made often, for lack of economic incentive.

Some people have attempted to make a case for some connection of the New World with the legend in Plato of the early "Atlantis" civilization. The two Platonic dialogues that record this tale are available in translation in convenient form in one paperback volume: *Timaeus and Critias*, New York: Penguin Books, 1983, translated by Desmond Lee. When we consider the story of Atlan-

# Beasts and Battles

tis, we should consider it from the point of view of an Egyptian, not of a person in Greece. For the story was brought back to Greece from Egypt. It tells of a sunken island (not continent) that was quite large, being of greater extent than Libya plus Asia (pp. 37-38). When ancient authors speak of "Asia", they often mean what we today would call Turkey. But, in any case, the island was large, and from it one could reach other islands, and from them reach a large (mysterious) continent. These were placed outside the Straits of Gibraltar (p. 37). A power arising from somewhere "out there" attempted to conquer the entire Mediterranean coast, but were held off by the Athenians (p. 38). But the Athenians then lost all their army in an earthquake, and the island of Atlantis was simultaneously swallowed up by the sea (p. 38). The story is said by Plato to be true, not fiction (p. 39).

It had been given to Solon, a famous Athenian lawmaker, on a visit to Egypt. The story purports to go back 9,000 years before the time of Solon (first half of the 6th century, B.C.); the 9,000 years (p. 131) is, of course, not possible. Many authors have suggested that there is an added zero, and that 900 years should be more reasonable; this does seem likely. There is an island that blew up, and part was lost to the sea: Santorini (or Thera); though this island is found in the Mediterranean, not outside the Straits. Nevertheless, this island is (when compared to Crete, where indeed the same people lived in the time before "Greece" arose to much notice), very suggestive of "Atlantis". If we look for simple things in common, we notice first of all the bull, which plays a role in rituals or entertainments of Cretan civilization and is also found in the Atlantis legend. And we see in the legend a portrayal of regular meetings of island princes; we know that there were many "kingdoms" on the island of Crete. Cretan art-work is very distinctive.

The wall paintings of Thera-Santorini are in the same style. Thucydides noted the civilization of Crete as having spread out through various islands and put down piracy by virtue of its navy (Modern Library edition, pp. 5, 7).

While the island of Thera did not sink, it did explode because of a terrific volcanic blast, which had been thought until recently could be dated to about 1450 B.C. (which does fit well with Solon's time plus 900 years). And, if one island was destroyed—reduced to a mere shell of itself—by a volcano, it is possible that some other one did in fact sink, within the Mediterranean.

# Discovering America

Whether there was another "victim" or not, it does seem that the civilization on Crete, the larger isle, was overthrown by some force, in order for the mainland Greeks to take control of at least parts of it.

One point to note: on the other side of the island of Thera is a continent larger than Libya and Asia put together. *From an Egyptian perspective,* that continent is Eurasia. (The "Libya" meant might be larger than the modern Libya; but the "Asia", probably meaning modern Turkey, is smaller; and both together are much smaller than the modern Eurasia.) Therefore, the island of Thera-Santorini matches well with the idea of a destroyed "Atlantis", although modern archaeological work indicates that the inhabitants of the island had warning of the volcano's coming eruption, and escaped before the disaster came about. Thera was not a huge island even before part of it was blown away by the volcano—but Crete is large, and it was obviously part (and probably the chief part), of the Minoan culture and civilization.

Although scholars have put the date of the explosion on Thera anytime between 1450 B.C. and 1500 B.C., there are some new claims for an older date. The *Science News* magazine of August 22, 1987, p. 121, notes a claim for a date of the explosion of about 1645 B.C. This date is based on analysis of Greenland ice core acidity. One might wonder whether such a study result might be unduly affected by volcanic action from nearby Iceland, but if the new date holds up, the neat fit with the presumed "900 years" of the age of the disaster from Solon's time will no longer exist.

We are becoming used to upsets in chronology. The "traditional" date of the Trojan War (if there was such a war), was 1190 or 1200 B.C.; but we now believe that was the time that the purported aggressors in that war were themselves overthrown.

Modern findings indicate that, except for the time, and except for the placement outside the Straits of Gibraltar, there do seem similarities that make the islands of Crete and Thera-Santorini seem candidates for parts of a possible "Atlantis" economic empire. The Minoans of Crete were very likely an earlier trading people somewhat on the order of the Phoenicians. They could have traded past the "Pillars of Herakles" (Straits of Gibraltar). And it is at least a possibility that there might be another casualty besides Thera. We know that an earthquake caused a part of a Portuguese port to sink with loss of life some two hundred years ago; it may well be that some island trading post or base in that area in early times had suffered a similar fate.

The attempt to conquer the entire Mediterranean coast seemed to be a doubtful reference until we learned about the so-called "Peoples of the Sea". About 1200 B.C. there were great dislocations around the eastern Mediterranean, and vast fleets of "pirates" (in Egyptian eyes) tried to conquer Egypt itself. Troy may have fallen a second time. Although these things happened some 250 years or more after the explosion on Thera, it would be easy to see how disparate large events might become combined in the memory of later years.

While there may be a vague memory of the Americas in the tale Plato told, we also have the option of "seeing through Egyptian eyes", and looking north from Egypt, past Thera, to Eurasia (Europe plus Asia being a huge continent, indeed). Few, if any, scholars believe in a Minoan discovery of America. Whether Minoan traders could have come across a tale of a distant continent across the Atlantic from early Irish explorers, seems doubtful. It is faintly possible—just barely possible—that Phoenician traders of a later day obtained such information somehow, and passed it on to Egyptian temple sources, with additions that would prevent competitors from trying to trade with England or the west coast of Portugal or France: someone said the passage out of the Mediterranean was blocked by the mud from the sunken island of Atlantis! (Plato, *op. cit.*, p. 38), and that tale survived a long time in ancient writings.

Whatever the early contacts of the "Old World" with the New, there was no really lasting contact until the time of Columbus' voyage, so far as we know. There are vague indications of an interesting nature, but the entire subject remains speculative at this date.

There are claims of very ancient habitation of people in the New World, but they have yet to be proved. For the time being, it seems we must suppose people to have entered the New World from Siberia sometime around 12,000 years ago, and gradually spread into South America; but we will keep alert to new evidence, and retain an open mind to the presentation of more ancient remains.

The "pyramids" of Central America are evidently native to the New World. They are more like the ziggurat type of structure in their temple function, although constructed of stone instead of mud brick. The Central America structures are apparently ceremonial in purpose, while the Egyptian pyramids are simply massive tombs. Since any ocean connection between Mesopotamia and Central America seems very unlikely, these Mayan and Aztec structures do seem to emphasize native effort. The Phoenicians would have known of the ziggurats surmounted by temples in Mesopotamia, and the Phoenicians shared the trait of human sacrifice with the peoples of ancient Mexico and Central America. But there are differences even in those factors: the Phoenicians sacrificed children predominently, while the Indians sacrificed adults. It would require much more than a vague and seldom-used trade-route link to motivate the erection of structures such as the pyramids of the New World.

# ◀ 14 ▶

# IPHICRATES' INVENTION?

When does confidence and *ésprit de corps* become the kind of blind arrogance that is dangerous to an armed force? When does cowardice become tactical intelligence? Somewhere within these limits may be found many a brilliant victory, and many a terrible defeat, and much is a matter of judgement. For a time the ancient Greeks had fought each other and their enemies with the use of heavy bronze protective armor. The head, chest, and shins were protected, and there was also the shield; this equipment was heavy but also advantageous. When meeting opponents not so armed, such as the Persian infantry, the Greeks had the advantage, and were generally victorious. Not only were they more impervious to sword or spear thrust, but they also were compelled to maintain good physical conditioning and athletic ability in order to simply carry the weight of their equipment.

The time was to come when this advantage could become so grave a disadvantage that the method of war based upon it would be shown to be obsolete. An Athenian general by the name of Iphicrates is often given credit for the way of war or "invention" that had that result. Though he is credited with the methods involved in various histories and especially military histories, the innovations were not his.

Sometimes new knowledge brings us to new possibilities of insight into things long thought to be nonsense, or perhaps viewed as superstitious stupidity. Into that category falls the scientific opinion of meteorites, or "stones that fall from the sky".

# Beasts and Battles

From the view that "there are no stones in the sky", to the opinion that meteorites do exist, our general opinion has followed a path from denial to acceptance: more or less because we finally bothered to look at the evidence. (There is a related subject that is still thought to be silly or nonexistent—the "thunderstone". Such stones were thought to fall from the sky preceded by a large crashing noise in the old days; since we now know of the so-called "sonic boom," should we not at least reserve judgement on this old-time category of strange or unusual things?)

When we look at the actual evidence for the "outmoding" of the fully armored Greek warrior, we note that in 390 B.C. the Spartan heavy-armed infantry to the number of about 600 were attacked near Corinth by lightly-armed javelin-men under the command of the general Iphicrates (Xenophon, *A History of My Times*, New York: Penguin Books, 1983 paperback, pp. 219-220; also known as the *Hellenica*). The javelin-men were told to go not much nearer the Sparatn enemy than the distance of a javelin throw, and to retreat quickly (run away) when the Spartans charged. Since the Spartans were weighed down by their armor, they could not come close to any of their enemy; and when they turned to go back to their ranks, they received more javelins from behind. This scene was repeated often, but with the same result. The javelin-throwing enemy also attacked the flanks, and especially the non-shielded side of the Spartans, and many were lost. The victory was designed by Iphicrates, and he does receive credit for it; and he could use such tactics again in the future when need arose. Here we have a professional soldier who used intelligent professional tactics. Should we class him with the great captains of war, and salute his genius?

Not necessarily. He may simply have been repeating a tactic that worked well and was noteworthy some thirty-seven years previously. It had worked again in a yet more famous case thirty-five years before.

The western area of northern Greece, called Aetolia, was thought of by the classical Greeks as being somewhat barbarous and not quite on the same level as the rest of the Hellenes (their own name for themselves). Demosthenes, the Athenian leader, invaded this area in 427 B.C., chiefly because it seemed to present a series of easy conquests.

This Demosthenes was a general, and not the famous orator

# Iphicrates' Invention?

of the same name who was active some three or four generations later at Athens. But Demosthenes the general was apparently an example of the Athenian predisposition towards great activity, as compared with the Spartan conservatism and lack of initiative.

Aetolia was an area located west of Athens but with its southern border being at the mouth of the Corinthian Gulf, the body of water that separated north and south Greece, except for the narrow join at the isthmus. Since Athens was a naval power, it would be somewhat convenient, though perhaps not vital, to be able to control the northern mouth of the Gulf. The Locrians, allies of Athens in the Peloponnesian War now being fought, were already situated upon areas of the north coast of the Gulf inside its mouth that opened to the western sea. The Locrians were on the north coast of the Gulf at its narrowest width, so that any strategic considerations should involve the Athenians aiming to simply retain the areas they already controlled. Thus the fortification and defense of Naupactus would be a worthwhile strategic aim for Athens, whereas obtaining a naval base at the (wide) mouth of the Gulf might be nice, but not really needed.

The warriors of the Greek cities of the time fought in much the same ways. Battles were decided by the push of spear-line against spear-line, with minimum light-armed help. The Athenians were strong heavy-armed fighters just as were the Spartans, and the Aetolian citizen-soldiers were not ready to face them in close combat. The tale of the campaign is found in *The Peloponnesian War* of Thucydides, New York: Modern Library edition, 1951, pp. 198-199. The lightly-armed javelin-men of the Aetolians were kept more or less at a distance by the archers on the Athenian side; but when they exhausted their supply of arrows, it became a different situation; the nimble Aetolian javelin-men could run close, throw their javelins at the Athenians, and then run away without harm as the heavy-armed Athenians tried to follow. Demosthenes suffered a disastrous defeat in the campaign.

This campaign also showed a certain lack of ability to concentrate on their real war aims on the part of the Athenians; the Aetolians were not Spartan allies, and the protracted Peloponnesian War had been in effect for some years when this campaign was undertaken. There is a certain similarity to the more famous later mistake of the Athenian Syracuse campaign—in both cases the places invaded were at best peripheral to what should have been the main effort, and much could be lost in either case. It would have been better to do nothing in both cases; though the Sicilian venture was much riskier, the Aetolian campaign showed a similar disdain for remaining on the main track of the war with Sparta. If nothing succeeds like success, nothing fails like failure, and all of Athens' allies were not firm in their allegiance.

Some two years later, the Athenians had trapped a Spartan garrison upon the small island of Sphacteria, located off the west coast of southern Greece, almost adjoining a neck of land projecting from the mainland. Southern Greece was predominantly Spartan in allegiance, and of course was Sparta's actual location. A naval power like Athens was not likely to march inland against a respected land power like Sparta, but would benefit from selected sites for naval bases spotted here and there around and outside the territory of Sparta and its allies. Such a place was Pylos, an elevated site at the end of the neck of land projecting from the mainland. The site was fairly small, and just north of the elongated island of Sphacteria, which was much larger than Pylos.

In the years immediately after his Aetolian defeat in 427 B.C., the general Demosthenes had retrieved his reputation by a series of successes against enemy forces, and it was he who fortified Pylos as a possible base of operations against south Greece. He had probably chosen Pylos to occupy instead of Sphacteria because the latter would have required a larger defense force because of its bigger area. Demosthenes' Athenians built stone walls at key places, and beat off subsequent Spartan attacks on the position.

The Spartans meantime had occupied the island to the south; and their troops there, in conjunction with their mainland forces near Pylos and some ships that they had brought to the scene, effectively had surrounded the Athenians at Pylos. Then a large fleet of Athenian ships appeared, and the tables were turned. Now the Spartans on the elongated island just south of Pylos were surrounded in their turn.

Back in Athens, the politician Cleon had been given the command of the Athenian forces after his criticism of the regular military leadership. Forced into command by his own brags, he chose Demosthenes as his co-general, and brought to the scene of action numerous troops. Many of these were the usual heavy-armed troops calls "hoplites", but in addition there were contin-

# Iphicrates' Invention?

gents of archers, javelin-men, and slingers. They would invade Sphacteria.

Cleon's brag had made it necessary that the Athenian forces land and fight the Spartans, for he had questioned the slowness of the action of the previous generals, saying that he was not afraid of the Spartans, and could kill or capture them instead of doing nothing. These comments had been made at a time when the Spartans were considered the world's best infantry by everyone, including the Athenians.

The Athenian forces landed without trouble on the island, and an accidental fire destroyed the trees and shrubs of much of the island, leaving the Spartan defenders no appreciable ground cover. The result would be to make missile attacks more effective as well as to prevent any chance of ambush by the defenders. The attacking troops were apparently under instructions from Demosthenes, with Cleon seemingly taking no part in planned tactics.

Demosthenes stationed some missile troops upon high places, in such a way that missiles would reach the enemy from different directions. Though his heavy-armed troops probably outnumbered the enemy, he seems to have ordered them to hang back and maintain their ranks in a defensive posture, without advancing. The remainder of the light-armed troops were instructed to run at the enemy, discharge their javelins, arrows, or stones from slings, and then to run away when the Spartans gave chase. By repeating such attacks, the light-armed troops wounded and killed the Spartans without suffering any harm in return. Thus, in 425 B.C., several years after receiving the same sorts of attacks in Aetolia, Demosthenes applied the lesson he had learned to such cost. The tactics that had worked against his Athenians in 427 B.C. worked against the Spartans in 425.

Weighed down in their heavy armor, the Spartans could do little. They could not catch their tormentors, and when they turned back to regain their ranks, they were hit with missiles in the back. Finally they retreated to an old stone fort. Some Athenian archers and light-armed troops secretly made their way to high ground in their rear, and on their appearing there, the Spartans expected to be killed. Their situation was hopeless, for now they were caught between missile fire from two directions, with the Athenian heavy infantry able to finish them after they were sufficiently weakened.

The Athenian leaders held back their troops, and offered

the remaining Spartans a chance to surrender. This was accepted after heralds were sent to the mainland to ask the opinion of the Spartans there. The historian Thucydides has this whole story (*op. cit.*, pp. 224-230, and especially p. 227). The Athenian side had few losses, because they and their allies had refused to come into close contact with the Spartan heavy-armed infantry and their allies (Thuc., p. 230). The tactics of Demosthenes had been a great success.

The Greek world was astonished at the outcome. The Spartan reputation of fighting to the death and of being invincible in battle was affected. Like the Persians after Marathon, the Spartans lost the aura of inevitable victory. The sacrifices of the "Aetolian lesson" had cost the lives of some of the "best men" of Athens (Thuc., p. 199), but now the lesson had been applied in a beneficial way. It may be that a chance to make the hardships and sacrifices of the Athenians even more meaningful was missed, for the result of the capture of Spartans at Sphacteria was that the Spartan state desired to get its men back and end the war. The Athenians refused the overtures, and eventually lost the war. There had been a series of conflicts with Sparta, and it may well be that a peace with neither side losing much would have only been of a short duration. Had such a peace lasted, however, history would have been different to perhaps a great extent: and the capture of Sphacteria made such an outcome at least possible.

A reasonable settlement between Athens and Sparta was not obtained, and the negotiations failed (Thuc., p. 231). The Athenians, concentrating on their own immediate environment, failed to recognize the long-term danger of Persian gold used against them. When that gold replaced a destroyed Spartan fleet, the way to Spartan victory was made feasible.

The tactics used in 427 B.C. by the Aetolians had probably been used by others before. Rather than being a brilliant new invention, the tactics represent the recognition of one's own weakness. A force unable to meet an enemy in the field directly has little else to do—other than simply to run away. The use of arrows, javelins, and sling-stones at a distance begins as a natural tactic for a weaker force facing a stronger one.

To place such tactics in one's repertory for use when convenient is the mark of a good military intelligence, which the Greeks certainly did not lack. But the production of these tactics to suit

## Iphicrates' Invention?

the occasion seems to be more an invention of the fifth century general Demosthenes than of the general Iphicrates. Perhaps Iphicrates is given the credit for the "invention" of the power of the light-armed against the heavy-armed because there were so many other factors impinging upon the important events at Pylos and Sphacteria—and because he used such tactics repeatedly. But a careful reading of Thucydides (*op. cit.*, pp. 198-199, and 227), shows where the method came into use against Demosthenes in 427 B.C., and where he used it himself in 425 B.C.—so that the later use in 390 B.C. by Iphicrates amounts to the copying of a famous event, and not the brilliant invention of something new in the military art.

Historians are beginning to see the importance of the role of Persia in the Peloponnesian War more clearly than they may have done in the past (for instance, *The Oxford History of the Classical World*, Boardman, Griffin, and Murray, editors; Oxford/New York: Oxford University Press, 1986, pp. 145, 195). Even more interesting than the way the Athenians seem to have ignored the dangers of Persian intervention in their affairs may be the way they appear to have ignored the possible use of large Phoenician fleets. And since those fleets were subjects and allies of Persia, it would seem dangerous to leave them out of account. There may be an unresolved mystery in that direction, awaiting some historian's answer.

# ◆ 15 ◆
# ATLANTIS AGAIN

It should be emphasized that the interpretation of remains of the past must to a great extent remain speculative. Such "interpretation" can never be an absolutely "hard" science. Yet there does seem to be some possibility of one's view of such remains being more or less probable.

We must not forget that we are in a different environment, with a heritage that differs from that of the peoples of the past. And, to add to our difficulties, we do not have a complete record of the past, whether in writing or in other remains. Our "cultural conditioning" or "mental set" is different. These difficulties are enough so that one could legitimately hold that it would be impossible to understand the past at all. But it is also possible to hold that an over-riding "basic nature" of people in general, combined with some minimum evidence remaining from the past, allows us to make interpretations about that past—though such interpretation will obviously range from "doubtful", through "possible", to "likely".

There are some remains that we are not likely to be able to understand at all. For instance, Sir Leonard Woolley, in his book *A Forgotten Kingdom* (Baltimore, a Penguin "Pelican" 1953 paperback), describes the digging of a deep shaft and its subsequently being filled with boulders (p. 44), some of which were quite heavy and brought from a considerable distance. Then, after the shaft was filled with stones, a wall was built over it, with one end resting upon it, and an altar was created nearby. While we cannot "know"

# Beasts and Battles

what such a thing was all about, we can accept Woolley's view that this business had something to do with religion (*ibid.*). We might go "out on a limb" and guess that the stones represent substitutes for human sacrifice; this seems to be at least possible, while a link to the Greek legend of Zeus being safeguarded by stones being fed to his "father" Kronos might be placed in the "doubtful" category. Further, it is true that there is an odd connection of people to stones in Greek legend—consider the peopling of the earth by the Greek flood survivors Deucalion and his wife, when they toss stones over their shoulders to produce people. Whether this "human sacrifice" interpretation is correct, or whether the inhabitants of the early Alalakh were simply creating, (and then blocking), a "door to the underworld", it remains true that there is enough evidence for human sacrifice and even for head-hunting in the prehistory of northern Europe to enable a scholar from New Guinea or Borneo to write several tomes upon the matter.

Be that as it may, we will now leave the ancients of Alalakh and their mysterious stone-filled shaft, and remark upon discoveries that the peoples of north-west Europe dug deep pits and buried therein lengthy trees. Other than the knowledge that the early peoples of Germany and Scandinavia held certain trees sacred, what can we make of this? It may be that one key is given us by the classical scholar Michael Grant. In his *The World of Rome* (New York, Meridian, 1987 paperback), he notes that the cult of Cybele/Attis in Rome involved a procession in which a newly cut pine tree was carried (p. 193) as part of colorful celebrations. Attis was the lover of Cybele, an Earth-Mother type, and this male figure died annually only to be re-born in the spring with the earth's vegetation; the relevance for people dependent upon agriculture is evident. The believers would mourn for a time, and then rejoice in the belief that Attis would "come back" next year, as it were. The "tree" represented him.

This goddess of many names in many lands probably goes back to the "Venus" figures of the Stone Age. But the point to make here is the *possible* link between a cult that entered Rome around 204 B.C. (cf. Grant, *op. cit.*), and more northern peoples dependent upon agriculture. It is tempting to see the spread of agriculture as being accompanied by religious rituals of some nature, and some may have been imported later. We know that human sacrifice took place in the north because of the preserved bodies found in Scandinavian bogs. But it is true that we don't know ritual details. And "tree burial" may not have substituted for people, but may have simply represented the male god figure, as in Grant's description of Rome's Cybele cult. The god Attis is similar to the god Osiris of Egypt, insofar as neither one is "really dead", although both had died.

While it is true that we have to allow for poetic imagination in the myths and legends of the peoples of the past, it should be said again that some things derive from descriptions of real people or events. To say that "all is mythic" or from some "collective unconscious" is just as much one-sided and erroneous as to say that everything is or was based in reality. As Herwig Wolfram remarked in his *History of the Goths* (Berkeley, University of California Press, 1988, p. 351), Saga elements can recall real historical events and people.

Every so often, odd coincidences catch our eye. One such is the common belief in early "created" peoples made from wood, found in both the Viking belief and the Mayan belief. Of course, "diffusionism" (the bringing of ideas from one people to another), remains a good deal out of fashion in the intellectual world of scholars today. But we know that the Vikings settled Iceland, went on to Greenland, and even ventured as far as the north of Newfoundland. While most of their activities took place in the far north, there is nothing that would have prevented some sailing south all the way to Central America.

The *Popol Vuh*, translated by Dennis Tedlock, and called "the definitive edition of the Mayan Book of the Dawn of Life," etc., on the book jacket (Tedlock, Dennis, *Popol Vuh*, New York: Simon and Schuster, 1985), contains a belief that an earlier race of people was created by the gods out of wood (*Popol Vuh*, pp. 80-86, esp. pp. 83, 84). Now compare the Norse belief as given by Gwyn Jones, where the gods made the "first man and woman" from "two trees, or a tree and creeper" (*A History of the Vikings*, Oxford: Oxford University Press, 1984, p. 317). Of course separate peoples living in woodlands might well come up with such conceptions separately, but people-to-people contact is not actually precluded.

To stretch the point of *possible* Viking-Mayan contact, there is an interesting description of a (presumably evil) parrot with blue teeth who is killed in the *Popol Vuh* (pp. 90-94 for this tale). Two

# Beasts and Battles

heroic Mayan youths destroy this creature named Seven Macaw, who loses his blue teeth when he dies (p. 93). The parrot had thought highly of himself until dying. Here rare blue teeth in the story catch one's eye immediately.

We think of the famous king of Denmark named Harald Bluetooth, who was converted to Christianity about 960 A.D. (Jones, *op. cit.*, p. 126), and who exerted his influence all the way to Norway to pressure Scandinavians to accept the religion and give up the old pagan ways. This was not liked by some, who preferred to emigrate to Iceland, and even Greenland. We know America was discovered between 986 A.D. and 1000 A.D. (c.f. Brøndsted, Johannes, *The Vikings*, translated by Kalle Skov; London: Penguin "Pelican" 1965 paperback; pp. 87, 111). And the "blue-toothed" parrot had a son who was exceptionally strong, and was found at the Mayan shore, whose name was "Zipacna" (*Popol Vuh*, pp. 94-97). Some of the Mediterranean peoples thought the Vikings even stronger than the Germans (and they probably were, since they rowed their long-boats when the wind was not available to fill the sail).

The above scenario of Vikings-meet-Mayans is not here presented in a serious manner meant to set forth an actual historical fact, but rather to demonstrate how easily one may construct connections from random facts of history. Some of what seem at first to be suggestive links are in fact nothing more than the merest coincidence, such as the (faulty) linking of the Cretan king-name "Minos" to the early Egyptian king-name "Menes"; there is no real connection. The constructed Viking-Mayan "link" may be no better, though it is not impossible.

The stone inscription called the "Kensington Stone" from Minnesota is apparently a hoaxer's attempt to create a "Viking inscription" on a stone in America, and a Viking presence in Minnesota. The fact of the hoax is said to be obvious to scholars of ancient languages. Erik Wahlgren, *The Vikings in America* (London: Thames and Hudson, 1986, pp. 100-105), has a good discussion of this hoax.

There are some things we should like to know. Such as: Do the English drive upon the left side of the street because Napoleon Bonaparte ordered everyone to pass on the right (as he in fact did)? And are the various tales of the "massacre of the first-born"

# Atlantis Again

in the Bible inspired by the real sacrifice by Phoenicians of their own children?

There was a river behind the ancient coastal town of Byblos that annually ran red with the blood (actually clay), of the dying/reviving god Adonis; did this inspire the story of Moses turning the Nile to blood? Adonis was a god like Attis, who would regenerate in the spring of the year.

We seem to be on somewhat firmer ground with the interpretation of the buried tree theme as representing some sort of male consort deity, who being "married" to the Earth Goddess was sometimes perhaps buried in the ground as part of a religious rite. Some sense would thus be lent to puzzling archaeological discoveries of the "tree in a pit" variety, and the pine tree Attis procession in the Roman Cybele rite seems to provide a possible explanation for an otherwise inexplicable thing.

We are on less firm ground with the ancient Greek tale of the princess Andromeda being put out for sacrifice to a dragon from the sea, in the Perseus rescue adventure. This tale seems to have come from Joppa, a few days' sail from Egypt. We know that in the time of Herodotus, the Egyptians kept tame crocodiles, which they fed and decorated with bracelets and ear-rings, and embalmed when they died (Herodotus, *Persian Wars*, Book II, Ch. 69). The town of Joppa on the coast of Palestine, in Greek days a Phoenician trading port, was in early days under the thumb of Egypt; and we wonder if in very ancient times people might have been fed to crocodiles in Egypt as sacrifices? Herodotus (Book II, Ch. 45), gives a tale which "the Greeks tell" about Herakles being led to sacrifice until he turned and slew the Egyptians around him. Herodotus denies this tale as anything but a silly fable, since in his time the Egyptians had no such practices (*Ibid.*). But, much earlier than Herodotus, some scholars believe that even kings might have been sacrificed.

In regard to the thought that "Atlantis" might really have been Crete (or Thera/Santorini, or both), Michael Grant points out an interesting item. If he is right in his belief that the Greeks thought of "Asia" as being only the part of western Asia Minor that made up the kingdom of Lydia (Grant, Michael, *The Ancient Mediterranean* (New York: Meridian Books, 1988 paperback, p. 86), then we might consider again the description of Atlantis as being larger than Asia and Libya together. We don't really know what the

## Beasts and Battles

sources meant by "Libya", though we know that not all of north Africa was meant. By "Libya" the Egyptian source may have meant a small slice of land such as that including the town of Cyrene and its immediate territory, to the west of Egypt. In any event, if the Greeks considered "Asia" to mean "Lydia" (instead of the Roman meaning of "Asia" as western Asia Minor), then an "Atlantis" island that was larger than Asia and Libya together would not be quite so large as we thought at first. And a sailor coasting along the southern shore of the island of Crete might consider that length to imply an island larger than, say, Lydia plus Cyrenaica.

Minoan Crete vanished, of course, under a combination of the ravages of nature and attack by Mycenaean type warriors ("vanishing" in this case meaning the stopping of trade). In addition to the destruction of the island Thera/Santorini by volcanic explosion, Grant reminds us that at least one sizable town at the southern tip of the Peloponnese (south Greece) sank beneath the waves at about the time of the Thera seismic catastrophe, and other towns may have been so affected (Grant, *The Ancient Mediterranean*, p. 99). The same event or events seem to have weakened Crete for foreign invasion, though it remained above water. It "vanished" as a Minoan place, and "reappeared" as a Mycenaean Greek place.

As mentioned in the previous Chapter 13, the sources describe "Atlantis" as an *island*, and not as a continent. A continent is mentioned, but it lies "on the other side" of, and past, Atlantis itself. Such a continent would be properly referred to as a lost continent *past* Atlantis, and not as a lost continent *of* Atlantis. As we noted before, the continental mass of *Eurasia* would certainly fit the description in the source, *when considered from an Egyptian point of view.* After all, the "continent" was not "lost"; the island of "Atlantis" was "lost"—it had dropped beneath the waves.

In the tale from Plato, the town of Athens is given a heroic part in standing against the invading forces that were attacking the Mediterranean shores, just before "Atlantis" sank (or, as we would say, Thera exploded). It is noteworthy that Athens seems to be about the only Mycenaean town that survived the various attacks that marked the beginning of the so-called "dark ages", and the end of the Mycenaean era. Granted that the Thera explosion took place about 1475 or 1450 B.C., and that the raids of the "Peoples of the Sea" took place at least 250 years later. But when

# Atlantis Again

we hear the story of "Atlantis" from Plato's report of the Egyptian priest's tale, it does seem that these two events are conflated. The tale may join events from centuries apart. The Peoples of the Sea were a confederacy, some of whom seem to have been "Keftiu" (a name for Cretans, according to some scholars). They attacked Egypt, and were defeated by Ramses III. Since Athens alone survived the Mycenaean era, one must wonder (despite the Egyptian priest's version of Athenian heroic resistance to the invaders), whether Athens' survival was due to its joining with the sea raiders instead of opposing them? Perhaps we do the ancient Athenians an injustice—it is difficult to determine. It is certainly true that mysteries remain about the fall of the Mycenaean strongholds with their massive stone walls, especially considering that the early Greeks had no real knowledge of seige warfare (which they still lacked even so late as the war between Athens and Sparta).

We have shown that, to the ancients, the description of a place larger than Asia and Libya together might be used of an island of fairly large size, while to us in the modern world, the meaning leads to a grotesque result because we use words like "Asia" to designate a different area. When we get closer to what seems reasonably to have been the original meaning, the ludicrous nature of the descriptions seem to no longer hold. Crete or Sicily are both large islands, and from either one Europe can be reached. Thera was never a very large island even before it exploded, but Crete was, and Crete was part of the same cultural complex. And, from Crete, one could indeed reach Eurasia by using intermediate islands as stepping stones, as in the old priest's tale. All things considered, a Minoan origin for the Atlantis story seems very likely.

That the days of Atlantis were considered as "superior" is not surprising. The idea of a past "golden age" is an understandable human product: sort of like talking about the "good old days", and how things have declined since.

Much in nature and history remains mysterious. For instance, can the ancient northern peoples have gotten the idea for the "Valkyries" less from the legend of the Amazons than from the various statues and many coins depicting the type of the "winged Victory" crowning rulers?

Yet past people and even some "New Age" writers want to make Atlantis evidence for past super civilizations or creations of "Space People". But perhaps we should worry less about the so-

# Beasts and Battles

called "New Age" ideas that we notice around us. If there can be reasonable explanations for such creatures as Beowulf's "dragon" and the "Medusa" of the ancient Greeks, then we do not really live in such an odd world after all.

The "New Age" is really an old story. It will have occurred to many people that the new beliefs in "channelling" are very similar to the old beliefs in "mediums"—the "seance" reborn in a new guise. Some New Age advocates hold that crystals have "magical" powers of one sort of another. But the upper-class women of the Franks in the 6th century seem to have worn rounded crystals hung from their girdles, perhaps as fertility talismans according to James (James, Edward, *The Franks*, New York: Basil Blackwell, 1988, pp. 152-153, pictured in Plate 32 on p. 153 of his work). These spherical crystals doubtless did them no harm.

Toward the end of the 12th century a warning went forth from a learned man that dangerous times were approaching and within a few years would be upon the world's people. John of Toledo had predicted a unique celestial event well in advance of its happening: if all the planets were to conjoin, what might it not mean? Many precautions were taken by those who came to hear of the prediction. From Constantinople, through Germany, and even to England, preparations were made against the awful future event. When 1186 A.D. came, the conjunction actually occurred—and nothing happened. (This even is summarized in Daniel Cohen's *Myths of the Space Age*, New York: Dodd, Mead & Co., 1967, pp. 15-16).

About eight hundred years later in the United States, it was said that a great New Age would soon begin when the planets would come into rare positions. People should gather on hill-tops to await the great time. Some did, the heavenly bodies came into their predicted positions—and nothing happened.

Perhaps Americans tend to look on the "bright side" of things. It is clear that the medieval sense of sinfulness had been lost.

# ► 16 ◄
# SPECULATION IN DARKNESS

Peoples far apart could envision the same sort of thing. After the Four Hundred Boys of the Mayan legend were killed by Zipacna (*Popol Vuh*, pp. 96-97), they evidently rose into the sky to become a heavenly constellation. And if Josephus is correct, Roman generals told their soldiers that if they died in battle they would become a star—as claimed by Titus during the siege of Jerusalem in the first century A.D. (cf. Josephus, *The Jewish War*, translated by G. A. Williamson, notes by E. Mary Smallwood; New York: Dorset Press, 1985, p. 340). The mythic Greek Orion seems to have become a number of stars.

But early peoples of Europe did not always keep such airy concerns. From the Irish saga heroes who collected the heads of their enemies, to the Scythians, who the scholar Michael Grant once called "mounted head-hunters" (in his *The Ancient Mediterranean*, p. 181), many early peoples had more down-to-earth concerns. The Germans and Scandinavians wanted the best of both worlds: the transporting of heroes to the hall of the gods where they could enjoy perpetual drinking and fighting in a long-continuing afterlife.

In Chapter 11, the seeming extraordinary survival of a concept through the ages was mentioned: the idea of the shaman's animal "spirit" psychic helper. For this idea to survive for thirty thousand years seems impossible; even the minimal fifteen thou-

# Beasts and Battles

sand for the drawing in the Lascaux Cave seems unusual. Of course, such ideas could be "rediscovered" from time to time through the ages, by very different peoples. One might expect such an idea to be found among the American Indian peoples, but its emergence in settled towns in connection with "witchcraft" beliefs does seem strange—a Stone Age idea come to town. The witch's "familiar" cat or frog or weasel is a sort of mental refugee out of a past age.

After the development of writing, it was always possible for later peoples to learn of odd tales from earlier writings. They would no longer have to engage in oft-repeated rituals that reinforced whatever ideas they wished to pass down to the next generation. And it is conceivable that in differing ages similar events, though odd, might take place. Some such might be suggested by reading of such an event in the past, or similar conditions might produce similar solutions to problems in various eras.

One example of this might be the tale of the "Vampire Knight" related in Chapter 1. Besides the tale of the Viking use of the device of a living man concealed in a coffin in order to enter and (with his following mourners), capture a town, there seems to be an even earlier tale from the first century A.D. It seems that during the Roman siege of Jerusalem, a certain Rabbi "Johanan ben Zakkai" escaped from the city by having himself carried out in a coffin (for this see Note 16, p. 453, of Josephus, *The Jewish War*). Whether this is the original of the Bohemond escape-in-a-coffin scheme or not is unknown. The Vikings had probably never heard of the Rabbi. The Byzantines, however, very likely might have known the tale. They preserved Roman writings as well as Greek, and the upper classes in Byzantine society often prided themselves on their classical learning and acquaintance with literature. It is possible, then, that Anna Comnena, daughter of the Byzantine Emperor and well educated in religious and secular literature, might know the tale of the "Rabbi's Escape" and attribute it to Bohemond to account for a "mysterious" escape from Byzantine forces. But it is equally likely that Bohemond (also spelled "Bohemund"), thought of his trick escape himself (see Chapter 1).

Risen from his coffin, this intransigent knight and war leader raised a force of followers to be led by him to fight again with the Byzantines. He travelled through Italy and France spreading tales of how the Byzantines had "betrayed" the Crusaders (cf. Ostro-

# Speculation in Darkness

gorsky, George, *History of the Byzantine State,* translated by Joan Hussey; Revised Edition; New Brunswick, N.J.: Yale University Press, 1969, p. 365). The Byzantines had naturally resisted the carving out of kingdoms from territory traditionally their own. The stories spread by Bohemond would have been one of the elements that, in conjunction with the machinations of the merchants and leaders of Venice, led to the later 13th century "Crusade" against Byzantium in which the city fell to the western war-lords. But Bohemond himself was out of luck. Gathering his followers, he crossed into Byzantium's "sphere of interest" to the northwest of Greece, campaigning in 1107 and 1108 A.D. In 1108 he was decisively beaten at the town of Dyrrachium (Ostrogorsky, *op. cit.,* p. 366). On swearing allegiance to the Emperor, he was actually allowed to keep Antioch (Ostrogorsky, *ibid.*), before leaving for Italy as mentioned in Chapter 1. He had failed to become Byzantine Emperor himself (independent and proud, western war-lords had unbounded ambition), but his career had made worse the existing distrust and obvious differences between the west and the Byzantines.

Even when we have written sources, we speculate in darkness when we approach the understanding of the past. We do not know if Bohemond really travelled in a coffin, or if the tale was inspired by the story of the "Rabbi's Escape", or by some unknown tale, or made up through creative imagination on the part of the story-teller. But we do know a lot, despite our limitations, and in some cases the archaeologists in conjunction with historians have helped us to know certain things better than did the people who actually lived in some eras. We can guess that the origin of the so-called "words of power" notable in the history of magical practice lies in the dim ages past when writing was first invented—from a time when only scribes were educated, and priests or rulers, and when those marks somehow conveyed information—and when one's "name" on a list was usually bad news. The words that early kings sent did contain power: by deciphering the markings (what we call writing), the king's will could be implemented at a distance—and all because of little marks in a row. The experts do not tell us this. We guess it, and it might be true.

The experts study the pollen from ancient sites, and the geology and even the climates from the past. And the study of fecal matter from the past can even show the expert much about

# Beasts and Battles

what was eaten long ago—and there are the fossils, of course. So we know that whale or dinosaur remains are just that, and not remains of "giants". But, while we gain much knowledge in these ways, the cultural meanings that people of long ago produced and held are continually receding from us into the mists of time. What is the meaning of the Twin Serpents in Greek myth and legend? Two serpents are sent against the child Herakles (Roman Hercules), which he crushes to death in his baby hands. Two "dragons"—considered to be pythons by the ancients—were sent to devour Laocoön. There are two serpents upon our modern medical symbol, received by us from the past. The little statuettes from Crete which we named "Medusa" in a previous chapter each held two serpents, one in each outstretched hand.

The only time two serpents are found together (other than attack), is when they mate: is that the secret of the theme of the Two Serpents? Or does it indicate completion, or unity, or signify something else? We have no idea. We know that serpents lead solitary and individual lives in the ordinary course of nature. Many crocodiles can be found gathered together, but not usually serpents. Some meanings will probably always elude us.

We no longer wish to become stars, or to live with or in them as in the thoughts of Titus and his Roman legions. For in our time, we know that the stars are actually suns, and enormously far away from us—so far, in fact, that it is impossible for anything to be "written in the stars" for us.

The ancient Greeks thought that the gods would punish those that profaned their temples. When the Persians were beseiging the Greek town of Potidaea, the sea suddenly withdrew from a weak spot of the town, the Persians began to cross the wet land that the sea left, in order to capture the town. But, when they were part of the way across, the sea suddenly came back much higher than before, and those that were not drowned like the Egyptians chasing Moses, were killed by the Potidaeans in boats (Herodotus, *The Persian Wars*, New York: Modern Library, no date, p. 648). This disaster for the Persians was ascribed by the Greeks to the Persian meddling with the temple and image of Poseidon, god of the sea. But we know the real cause: that event describes what we would call a *tsunami*—a tidal wave. Caused by seismic forces, these waves first leave the off-shore bare, and then return with much more height than any ordinary wave, and can cause

# Speculation in Darkness

great damage and loss of life if people are caught unaware by them. So, when the sea washed over the attacking Persians at Potidaea, we can see a natural cause of that disaster, whereas the ancient peoples were only able to see religious manifestations. Our knowledge may be limited in many ways, but sometimes we have the capability, as in this case, of knowing more about an ancient event than do the people that experienced it. As our modern knowledge grows, we hope to learn from the events of the past, and to profit from their lessons.

# NOTES

*Chapter 4*

1. Date of 1136 A.D. from Introduction (p. x) to Sir Thomas Malory's *Le Morte d'Arthur*, Vol. 1, Penguin Books, New York, 1977, (paperback).
2. Barber, Richard, *King Arthur: Hero and Legend*, St. Martin's Press, New York, 1986 edition, p. 47. This book is an excellent survey of the history of the Arthurian tales, written by the editor of the annual *Arthurian Literature.*
3. *Ibid.*, p. 56.
4. *Ibid.*, p. 71.
5. *Ibid.*
6. *Ibid.*, p. 73.
7. Malory, Sir Thomas, *Le Morte d'Arthur*, Vol. 1, Penguin Books, New York, 1977, p. x of Introduction.
8. Barber, *op. cit.*, p. 117.
9. Gillingham, John, *Richard the Lionheart*, Times Books, New York, 1978, pp. 122-124.
10. *Ibid.*, p. 123. Richard, riding ahead of his forces in his war with his father, was met by William Marshal in the latter's determination to hold off the pursuit of Henry II; as Richard was not wearing armor, he appealed to William on that ground to desist from killing him. William then ran his horse through with his lance, sparing Richard but killing Richard's horse.
11. Malory, *op. cit.*, Vol. 2, e.g. p. 189 " . . . best knight" etc.; also cf. p. 530. It is an interesting coincidence that Duby calls William "The Flower of Chivalry" in the title of his book, while Richard Barber uses exactly this phrase to describe Sir Lancelot as conceived by Malory (Barber, *op. cit.*, p. 121).

# BIBLIOGRAPHY

*Chapter 4*

Barber, Richard, *King Arthur: Hero and Legend*, St. Martin's Press, New York, 1986.

Duby, Georges, *William Marshal: The Flower of Chivalry*, Pantheon Books, New York, 1985, (translation by Richard Howard).

Geoffrey of Monmouth, *The History of the Kings of Britain*, Penguin Books, New York, 1982, (translation by Lewis Thorpe), paperback.

Gillingham, John, *Richard the Lionheart*, Times Books, New York, 1978.

Malory, Sir Thomas, *Le Morte d'Arthur*, 2 Vols., Penguin Books, New York, 1977 (Introduction by John Lawlor), paperback.


*Chapter 5*

Arrian, 1984, *The Campaigns of Alexander* (translation by Aubrey de Selincourt). New York: Penguin Books (paperback).

Creasy, Edward Shepherd, 1987, *Fifteen Decisive Battles of the World*. New York: Dorset Press; (reissue of an 1852 edition).

Engels, Donald W., 1980, *Alexander the Great and the Logistics of the Macedonian Army*. Berkeley: University of California Press (paperback).

Fox, Robin Lane, 1974, *Alexander the Great*. New York: Dial Press.

Fuller, Gen. John F., Ret., 1981, *The Generalship of Alexander the Great*. Westport: Greenwood Press; (reprint of 1960 edition).

Plutarch (No date listed), *The Lives of the Noble Grecians and Romans*. New York: Modern Library by Random House; (Dryden translation, revised by Arthur Hugh Clough).

Rufus, Quintus Curtius, 1984, *The History of Alexander* (translation by John Yardley). New York: Penguin Books (paperback).

Tarn, W. W., 1971, *Alexander the Great*. Boston: Beacon Press (paperback).

# Bibliography

Wilcken, Ulrich, 1967, *Alexander the Great* (translation by G. C. Richards). New York: W. W. Norton (paperback).


*Chapter 8*

Anonymous, 1963, *Beowulf* (translation by Burton Raffel). New York: New American Library (paperback).

Aune, Peter, *et al.*, 1983, *Scientific American* magazine article "The Stave Churches of Norway," August, pp. 96-105.

Barber, Richard, 1986, *King Arthur: Hero and Legend.* New York: St. Martin's Press.

Blair, Peter Hunter, 1966, *Roman Britain and Early England: 55 B.C.–A.D. 871.* New York/London: W. W. Norton & Co. (paperback).

Cohen, Daniel, 1970, *A Modern Look at Monsters.* New York: Dodd, Mead & Co.

Comnena, Anna, 1985, *The Alexiad of Anna Comnena* (translation by E. R. A. Sewter). New York: Penguin Books (paperback).

Cottrell, Leonard, 1968, *The Bull of Minos.* New York: Holt, Rinehart and Winston.

Davidson, H. R. Ellis, 1984, *Gods and Myths of Northern Europe.* New York: Penguin Books (paperback).

Derry, Thomas Kingston, 1979, *A History of Scandinavia.* Minneapolis: University of Minnesota Press.

Frost, Honor, 1987, *Natural History* magazine article "How Carthage Lost the Sea," December, pp. 58-67.

Guerdan, Rene, 1962, *Byzantium* (translation by D. L. B. Hartley). New York: Capricorn Books (paperback).

Horace, 1936, *The Complete Works of Horace* (C. J. Kraemer, Jr., Editor). New York: Modern Library by Random House.

James, Edward, 1988, *The Franks.* Oxford/New York: Basil Blackwell.

Jones, Gwyn, 1984, *A History of the Vikings.* Oxford/New York: Oxford University Press.

Newman, Paul, 1979, *The Hill of the Dragon.* Bath: Kingsmead Press.

Psellus, Michael, 1984, *Fourteen Byzantine Rulers* (translation by E. R. A. Sewter). New York: Penguin Books (paperback).

# Beasts and Battles

Raffel, Burton (See "anonymous" listing above, and "Troyes" below).

Renfrew, Colin, 1973, *Before Civilization: The Radiocarbon Revolution and Prehistoric Europe.* New York: Alfred A. Knopf.

Sturluson, Snorri, 1986, *King Harald's Saga* (from *Heimskringla*), translation by Magnus Magnusson and Hermann Pálsson. New York: Dorset Press.

Tonnelat, E., 1968, *New LaRousse Encyclopedia of Mythology*, article "Teutonic Mythology." New York: Prometheus Press. (Treats Scandinavian belief despite its title).

Troyes, Chrétien de, 1987, *Yvain, The Knight of the Lion* (translation by Burton Raffel). New Haven/London: Yale University Press.

Villehardouin, 1984, *Chronicle* (from *Joinville & Villehardouin, Chronicles of the Crusades*), translation by M. R. B. Shaw. New York: Penguin Books (paperback).

Wahlgren, Erik, 1986, *The Vikings and America.* London: Thames and Hudson.

Wolfram, Herwig, 1988, *History of the Goths.* Berkeley/London: University of California Press, (rev. from the second German edition).

Wood, Michael, 1987, *In Search of the Dark Ages.* New York/Oxford: Facts On File Publications. (Not to be confused with Hollywood television programs).

# SUGGESTED READING

*Chapter 10*

de Camp, L. Sprague, *The Fringe of the Unknown*, Prometheus Books, Buffalo, 1983 paperback, p. 14.

Landels, J. G., *Engineering in the Ancient World*, University of California Press, Berkeley, 1978, p. 206 (from Hero of Alexandria's surviving work; movement of heavy stones on sledges).

*Chapter 13*

## Bibliography

Wahlgren, Erik, *The Vikings and America*. New York: Thames and Hudson, 1986.

*Chapter 16*

Grant, Michael, *The Ancient Mediterranean*, New York: Meridian Books of New American Library, 1988 paperback.

Herodotus, *The Persian Wars*, translated by George Rawlinson, New York: The Modern Library, no date.

Tedlock, Dennis, translator, *Popol Vuh*, New York: Simon and Schuster, 1985.

# AUTHOR'S NOTE

The material in Chapters 7 and 8 was essentially worked out in 1959, and only now sees print. Some of the other material is of quite recent origin. The very interesting article of Wolinski only appeared in 1987, and gives rise to the possibility that ancient Rome left to us a legacy of three Masks instead of two: The Mask of Comedy, the Mask of Tragedy, and the Mask of the Werewolf

It should be emphasized that the contentions held in this volume are matters of *probability* and not matters of "proof."

—H. H. Trotti